ADVANCE PRAISE

"A must-read for leaders at all levels who want to move beyond fear-based beliefs to create teams and organizations shaped by purpose. A great resource for those in search of meaning at work in the twenty-first century."

—AMY C. EDMONDSON, NOVARTIS PROFESSOR OF LEADERSHIP AND MANAGEMENT AT HARVARD BUSINESS SCHOOL AND AUTHOR OF *BUILDING THE FUTURE: BIG TEAMING FOR AUDACIOUS INNOVATION* (BERRETT-KOEHLER, 2016)

"The Evolved Executive provides a thoughtful and provocative blueprint for the future of leadership and organizations. A must-read for any enlightened leader."

—DR. TASHA EURICH, PRINCIPAL OF THE THE EURICH GROUP; *NEW YORK TIMES* BEST-SELLING AUTHOR OF *INSIGHT* AND *BANKABLE LEADERSHIP*; AND PROUD MEMBER OF THE MARSHALL GOLDSMITH 100 COACHES PROJECT

"*This book is a must-read for any leader or executive who comes to work daily knowing there is a better and more purpose-derived way to serve the people who serve our patients and other customers. The quiet and not-so-quiet desperation for a path that is absent from today's disconnected workplaces is the subject of this book. It is written with heart from a leader with a heart...who has seen this type of leadership done well and also lived through and alongside the opposite. It is my hope that this practical body of work will become the way we lead and that we will do so unabashedly and even proudly. It will make a difference in our health: mind, body, and soul.*"

—JANDEL T. ALLEN-DAVIS, MD, VICE PRESIDENT OF GOVERNMENT, EXTERNAL RELATIONS, AND RESEARCH AT KAISER PERMANENTE

Allison,

THE EVOLVED EXECUTIVE

I hope you choose love,
even when it feels
a little scary!

Much love,
   Heather

The

Evolved

Executive

THE FUTURE OF WORK

IS LOVE IN ACTION

HEATHER HANSON WICKMAN PH.D.

LIONCREST
PUBLISHING

THE EVOLVED EXECUTIVE

The Future of Work Is Love in Action

ISBN   978-1-5445-1137-5 *Paperback*
       978-1-5445-1138-2 *Ebook*

Contents

Introduction

Let me begin by painting a quick picture.

- "Many workplace practices are as harmful as second-hand smoke."[1]
- "Workplace environments in the United States may be responsible for 120,000 excess deaths per year—which would make workplaces the fifth leading cause of death—and account for about $180 billion in additional health-care expenditures, approximately 8 percent of the total health-care spending."[2]
- Job stress costs US employers more than $300 billion annually.[3]

---

1   Jeffrey Pfeffer, *Dying for a Paycheck* (New York: HarperCollins, 2018), 50.

2   Pfeffer, *Dying for a Paycheck*, 43.

3   "Workplace Stress," The American Institute of Stress, accessed April 17, 2018, https://www.stress.org/workplace-stress/.

- Seventy-nine percent of people who quit their jobs cite lack of appreciation as their reason for leaving.[4]
- "According to the Mayo Clinic, the person you report to at work is more important for your health than your family doctor."[5]
- Fifty-eight percent of employees say they trust strangers more than their boss.[6]
- A whopping 73 percent of those surveyed say they work strictly for the paycheck.[7]

Last, but certainly not least...

- Fifty-eight percent of managers say they did not receive any management training whatsoever.[8]

These staggering statistics illustrate the severity of the current crisis of suffering in the world of work. Most of us spend the vast majority of our lives at work, and what we give is infinitely greater than just our time and energy. Research shows what many of us already instinctively

---

4   David Sturt and Todd Nordstrom, "10 Shocking Workplace Stats You Need to Know," Forbes.com, accessed April 17, 2018, https://www.forbes.com/sites/davidsturt/2018/03/08/10-shocking-workplace-stats-you-need-to-know/#50430534f3af.

5   Pfeffer, *Dying for a Paycheck*, 15.

6   Sturt and Nordstrom, "10 Shocking Workplace Stats You Need to Know."

7   "9 Reasons Americans Increasingly Hate Their Jobs," *Houston Chronicle* (online edition), November 2, 2013, https://www.chron.com/jobs/salary/article/9-Reasons-Americans-Increasingly-Hate-Their-Jobs-4957045.php.

8   Sturt and Nordstrom, "10 Shocking Workplace Stats You Need to Know."

know: the way we work isn't working anymore. We leave work with less energy, less confidence in our skills and ability, and more frustration. Now we have confirmed research on the toll all of this stress and suffering takes on our health and well-being. As Jeffrey Pfeffer finds, we are literally dying for a paycheck.

Take a step back and simply reflect on the language you hear at work. These likely sound familiar: "She threw me under the bus," or "He stabbed me in the back." How about our everyday use of "targets," "pick your battles," "marshalling resources," "command and control," and even "execution?" Language is powerful. Our words shape our experience and reflect our thinking patterns and beliefs. By taking a quick glance at our language, we can clearly see how we are filling the workplace with words of war and violence. What would our environment look like if it was filled with metaphors of love and collaboration?

This crisis of suffering occurs at all levels of the organization. People often look at those at the senior level or near the C-suite and imagine work is less brutal there. Unfortunately, that is also not the case. There's quiet, pervasive suffering at this level as well. Executives feel they must constantly prove themselves, never feeling psychologically safe. Worse, when executives feel the pressure to have all the answers, they hold back vital information, fail to consult, and actively block others for fear they'll lose their position or perceived authority. The company and the executives themselves suffer from harmful competition and ego, wasted time and effort that could be spent on any number of more useful things. Unfortunately, these patterns ripple through the entire organization like a heavy rock dropped into a pond.

Fortunately, there are profoundly better ways of working. The suffering isn't necessary! The old ways of management that brought us here aren't working for the new world of work, but we can and will evolve beyond them. This book is about embracing our own evolution and the evolution of our leadership beliefs, practices, and organizations. In the following pages, I will offer deep insight into the beliefs and skills that will need to change, provide intentional practices to adopt, and describe case studies of organizations who have already successfully made the leap. Evolved Executives and organizations not only thrive in the new world, often showing significant performance improvement compared to traditional organizations, but they do so while bringing purpose, meaning, and human connection to their employees and communities.

From my years climbing the corporate ladder, I've seen firsthand the suffering at work, but from my training in academia and my firsthand experience working with executives and leaders at evolving organizations, I can say with certainty there is a better way.

LOVE IN ACTION

The difference between organizations that exhibit this crisis of suffering and those whose people experience joy and meaning in their work is the difference between fear and love.

As many have said, there are only two basic human emotions—love and fear. Anything else falls into one of those categories. While we often talk about fear, in the workplace we almost never talk about *love*. In fact, many people get uneasy when it's used in this context. But to love is human. We all want to experience the feeling that we belong, that we are valued, that we are trusted to make important contributions at work. That, in its most basic sense, is love.

When you hear "love," don't think of romance. Think instead about three important ingredients.

First, love is the absence of fear. I'm reminded of a great quote from the book *Driving Fear Out of the Workplace*: "Fear doesn't motivate towards constructive action. On the contrary, it nourishes competition within an organization, fosters short-term thinking, destroys trust, erodes joy and pride in the work, stifles innovation and distorts communication."[9] The fear here—and its consequences—is

---

9   Kathleen D. Ryan and Daniel K. Oestreich, *Driving Fear Out of the Workplace: Creating the High-Trust, High-Performing Organizations* (San Francisco: Jossey Bass Inc., 1998), xiii.

what we see in a typical organization. But removing fear is only half the equation. Embracing love, the beliefs that foster love, the practices that embody love, and the words that share love, is where the magic resides for building organizations of the future.

Second, love, according to author Peter Block, is also the act of confronting people with their own freedom and autonomy. "What greater gift can you give someone than the experience of their own power, the experience that they have the capacity to create the world?"[10]

Lastly, love is about building caring, human connections in the workplace. It's about treating people with compassion, valuing their contributions, and honoring our full selves authentically at work. Oftentimes, in our fear, we think we can't get too close or know our employees because someday we might have to terminate or discipline them (watch the warlike parental language here again). Because of fear, we then don't create caring environments. We lose the opportunity to be human at work and end up numbing out a part of our soul, which serves no one.

I choose "love" on purpose, despite the reaction it often creates in so many people. In my heart, I know it's possible to create a more healthy and soulful world of work. Those

---

10 Peter Block, "Servant Leadership: Creating an Alternative Future," The Leadership Mind, March 30, 2008, http://leadershipdiamond.blogspot.com/2008/03/peter-block-servant-leadership.html.

close to me know I have been tempted to tone down my language. To not actually call it love for fear that it may repel readers. Or to make it more aligned with popular literature with words we are all more comfortable hearing. A choice to do so would be a violation of what I hold as my truth. In my heart, I know there is a world of work that fuels the mind, body, and spirit. One that connects us to an awe-inspiring shared vision that can literally change the world for the better. One that pushes us to grow and explore the edges of who we are and what our greatest potential truly could be. One that creates true and honest connectedness in service of the greater good. One that begins with love in action.

This perspective I hold regarding work did not come easy.

MY JOURNEY WITH LOVE IN ACTION

I am a classic achiever type, clearly Type A. I went all out in school, moving swiftly through undergrad, a highly ranked master's degree program in my field, and finally on to earn my doctoral degree. All this before I turned thirty-two, while working full time earning a six-figure salary. However, please know I don't share this to gloat but to simply show how drive can at times drown out important life messages. On the outside, it looked like I was on the path to big success, but internally, a nasty battle was brewing under the surface.

By the time I finished my PhD, I was serving in a senior-director-level position. I noticed this nagging, sinking feeling I just couldn't shake. From the outside looking in, I had everything I had worked so hard to achieve. I was working with the top executives of a big organization. I was part of a team doing incredible organizational redesign work and was offered the seemingly perfect next job in my climb. Yet, I was totally miserable. My soul was aching, and I felt a disconnect between the seemingly perfect path I was on and my heart and soul telling me every second that I wasn't doing what I was put on earth to do.

I worked in healthcare, where the values of providing health and care to patients are all about service. The higher up I got in these healthcare organizations, the more disconnected we were from those core values. It became about money, control, ego, and bureaucracy. It was critical to realize for myself that I was no longer in alignment with where I needed to be and how I needed to operate going forward. But I continued on.

Over the course of the next year, my marriage fell apart, I became more and more miserable in my roles at work and ended up increasingly burned out and depressed. In a last-ditch effort to find my way out of this feeling, I accepted a promotion from a dear friend and colleague to take on a new role in a new city. I lasted a year and a half before I cracked.

I remember lying in bed saying to myself, "There has got to be a better way!" I was witness to intense suffering at work—in my colleagues, my bosses, my teammates, in myself. I saw the workplace sucking the soul and energy out of the best laid plans and most beautiful people.

Shortly thereafter, everything I thought I believed in and everything I had striven to create no longer meant anything to me. I resigned and left the country for several months to find myself again.

I realized that no matter how disappointing, sad, and frustrating I found it to work at these organizations, they were doing the best they could with the knowledge and tools they had. So often, leaders don't have the mindsets, skillsets, or heartsets needed to lead soulfully in today's world. It's no fault of our own. We don't know what we need to know.

As I've come to learn, the universe has a fabulous way of teaching us lessons—repeating the lesson over and over, in greater magnitude, until it is learned. If this book teaches you nothing else, walk away with this. Pay attention when the voice is quiet, when it's early, when the lesson is manageable. If you wait, the lesson will get louder and louder until it destroys whatever part of your world is required for you to finally pay attention.

WHY LEADERS?

The general rule seems to be that the level of consciousness of an organization cannot exceed the level of consciousness of its leader.

—FREDERIC LALOUX, REINVENTING ORGANIZATIONS[11]

To evolve as organizations, we first need evolved leaders. Leaders who have developed beyond the needs of command and control management, who can take an honest look in the mirror and recognize that they first must be the change, and who can genuinely foster love, care, and humanness in the workplace. This is no small task, considering so many individuals have so little training or development on what it takes to be an effective leader.

Thankfully, the world is hungry for this change. So many people are asking for ways out of the suffering: "How can I increase engagement in my teams?" "How can I find more meaning, more connection, more fulfillment in my work?" Leaders are in a unique position to create immense change. However, to do so requires deep levels of growth, willingness to experiment with new ways of being, and the risk of losing what we once held dear.

I've lived in organizations that suck the soul out of us, places fraught with secrecy, gossip, toxicity, and suffer-

---

11   Frederic Laloux, *Reinventing Organizations: A Guide to Creating Organizations Inspired by the Next Stage of Human Consciousness* (Brussels, Belgium: Nelson Parker, 2014), 295.

ing. I've also been a part of organizations that are full of life, energy, love, and compassion and are genuinely thriving in terms of growth, profit, and revenue. This type of culture might have many names: purpose-driven, love-based, people-centered, human-centered. I'm here to ensure the evolution into this culture of love and health continues to grow.

A DIFFICULT BUT MEANINGFUL PATH

Growth is not an easy path. Sometimes, the easy path, the path of least resistance, is to continue in a job where you're suffering, getting your paycheck while slowly dying inside. That's not the path I want for you. I want you to grow into the new world full of fulfillment, meaning, and life. The road is not easy, but the destination is more than worth the effort—if you are willing to give up the good for the great.

To create soulful and meaningful organizations, we must grow as leaders. We must be willing to grow and risk on personal levels. We must be willing to make the purposeful choice to do something different and to do so in the face of great uncertainty. More significantly, we must chart a course as leaders when we ourselves cannot see the road beyond the next bend in the path. I push my coaching clients hard to think deeply about what risks they can allow themselves to take in pursuit of a different outcome.

Author Caroline Myss has said, "Choice is a fundamental power of the human experience."[12] Often the most powerful choices are the tiny ones, the ones that make small adjustments in how we show up, how we empower ourselves, and how we sabotage or betray ourselves. We are often terrified of choices and their consequences, but choices—especially difficult ones—can transform your life, your team, and your organization.

I am so grateful, in the end, to have gone through my own personal crisis. I saw firsthand what isn't working in the workplace, and I now have the opportunity to bring my knowledge and insight to leaders of organizations who want to embrace a new way of working. This way is propelled by their own evolution as a leader and powered by love in action.

As author and practitioner C. Otto Scharmer says, "What is at stake is nothing less than the choice of who we are, who we want to be, and what story of the future we want to participate in."[13]

Are you ready?

---

12   Caroline Myss, "Choices That Can Change Your Life," April 3, 2017, recorded at
      TEDxFindhornSalon, video, 25:55, https://www.youtube.com/watch?v=-KysuBl2m_w&vl=en.

13   C. Otto Scharmer. *Theory U: Leading from the Future as It Emerges* (Oakland, CA, Berrett-
      Koehler Publishers, Inc.), 92.

PART I

Where We Are and Where to Go Next

CHAPTER ONE

The Dilemma: How Did We Get Here?

Organizations are on the cusp of massive change as the world moves in more volatile, unpredictable, and uncertain ways. "The average lifespan of a company listed in the S&P 500 index of leading US companies has decreased by more than 50 years in the last century, from 67 years in the 1920s to just 15 years today."[1] Not only are companies failing sooner, but the rate of failure is also increasing. Can you imagine what it could look like in 2020 if we don't change our trajectory? Professor Richard Foster at Yale estimates by then, more than three-quarters of the current S&P 500 will not be there.[2] This is better known as the Fortune 500 disease:

---

1   Kim Gittleson, "Can a Company Live Forever?" *BBC News*, Business, accessed April 17, 2018, http://www.bbc.com/news/business-16611040.

2   Gittleson, "Can a Company Live Forever?"

The Fortune 500 Disease

The 'Fortune 500 disease' refers to the 90% of the companies on the original (1955) Fortune 500 list that are no longer on it. They have been unable to weather the disruptions of the last six decades. This suggests that big enterprises can't easily survive in the long-term.

One might conclude that many of the current Fortune 500 will soon be replaced by novel companies, and maybe by companies from emerging markets and industries. This will happen if they don't transform themselves successfully in time. It's a clear result of the demanding, dynamic character of an increasingly user-oriented market economy.[3]

For organizations to survive, we need more adaptable leaders capable of moving us to the next stages. We need a greater awareness and consciousness beyond simple black-and-white, quarterly report, profit-and-loss thinking. We must shift our ability to comprehend and deal with complex information that changes over time. Responsive and agile organizations, conscious capitalism, and conscious leadership all hold a basic truth: people and purpose matter just as much as profit, and possibly even more.

---

3   "Picking the Brain of the World's Most Radical CEO: Zhang Ruimin," Corporate Rebels, March 25, 2018, https://corporate-rebels.com/interview-zhang-ruimin/.

Unfortunately, many MBA schools in the country will still tell you that organizations exist solely to maximize shareholder value, meaning profit. Over the last few decades, it's become clear how problematic this worldview is.

The emphasis on profit alone, the high rate of failing companies, and the tremendous suffering that exists at work are all clear signs of the struggle we see in organizations. However, these aren't the only signs.

SIGNS OF THE STRUGGLE

I've worked with leaders across the United States, and some globally, who tell stories about their suffering at work. Often, they talk about coercion, being forced to betray themselves for the "good of the organization," and feeling dismissed and devalued.

Sometimes their suffering takes the form of seemingly small betrayals. For example, not being able to speak truth because of fear of losing one's job. Not speaking up in meetings for fear of being publicly humiliated or yelled at. Hiding behind a mask at work. Over time, each small betrayal adds up until the weight of them becomes overwhelming.

STORIES OF SUFFERING

I often hear stories from clients that truly illuminate the depth of the crisis we are facing in the workplace. Here are a few examples of those I hear most often.

SECRECY

Imagine walking into work on a Monday morning and feeling a palpable animosity in the air. Senior management has once again begun the week with a Monday morning closed-door meeting. You notice how they're careful not to speak until the door is closed and the shades are drawn. Everyone in the organization knows performance goals are set at the Monday morning meeting, but no one outside the meeting is "authorized" to know what they are. Management choreographs secrecy and weaponizes information against you.

TOXIC COMPETITION

Your new manager makes a habit of pitting you against another colleague for the sake of "healthy" competition. She gives you both similar assignments, telling you she wants to see who comes up with the best results in the shortest period of time. You feel intense stress and cutthroat competition, and both of you slide into destructive behaviors without meaning to, hoarding information and working to sabotage the other's progress when you can.

Not only do you hate working this way, but you know the survival-of-the-fittest games lead to duplicated, lower-quality work that doesn't take multiple perspectives into account. When you suggest working with your colleague next time instead of against him, your manager says it will take too much time and make you lazy.

JUST FIRE HIM

You are in a meeting with your senior executive colleagues discussing an individual about to be promoted to a very senior position. The individual hasn't yet signed the agreement for the position due to the fact he has a few additional questions. As the leadership team talks about the situation, the CEO simply says, "If he's going to ask questions, fire him." Others around the table stop and ask why they couldn't just answer a few questions. The CEO repeats, "If he's not going to sign the document, just fire him," and the new hire is fired. All of the time and energy put into the hiring process was just wasted and, worse, results in a toxic environment for the rest of you. The next time you have questions for the CEO, are you going to ask them?

GOLDEN HANDCUFFS

Your boss has started paying you large amounts of money to give up important aspects of your life. Just last week, he promised you a $10,000 bonus with the expectation that you forget about your family for the next month and concentrate on work. You missed your child's birthday. You'll miss her most important soccer games these next weeks and any time with your spouse, and you already regret accepting. Fear-based organizations use money to trump corporate values, and over time, they give out more and more money to convince people to sacrifice their values, too. This takes a huge toll on our souls and on our ability to live fulfilling lives.

FAKE FEEDBACK

Many corporations like to say they're "feedback-rich environments," where they both give feedback freely and welcome feedback by others. That sounds like a positive and healthy situation, but behind the talk, there's often dysfunctional dynamics. Feedback comes down from leaders just fine, but when you start sharing feedback up the chain of command, they shut you down. Worse, at the last meeting, your manager screamed at you, called you immature and ignorant, and reprimanded you. What did you do to deserve all of that? Simply sharing an opinion after it was invited, and it's not like this was an isolated event. No matter what kind of feedback the company says they're comfortable with, their actions make their true intentions and power relationships very clear. Actions always speak louder than words.

＊ ＊ ＊

Unfortunately, in these situations, everyone loses. Instead of transparent practices, secrecy is the norm. Instead of honesty, feedback is withheld or employees are reprimanded. Instead of valuing an integrated life, work is expected to trump all else. Even worse, leaders make failed attempts to add in caring gestures to the mix, which only confuses workers even more. People don't know which personality is showing up and which behaviors can actually be trusted. Is this going to be a caring adult conversation or a dysfunctional paternalistic correction?

These tactics may seem to work in the short term, but in the long term, they breed fear, resentment, and toxic burnout.

STUCK IN THE INDUSTRIAL REVOLUTION

So the question remains, how did we get here and why do we act the way that we do at work? There's a common saying in the field of healthcare: "Every system is perfectly designed to get the results that it gets."[4] The system we have now was built for the Industrial Revolution, and its

---

4   Attributed to several authors, most commonly W. Edward Deming. For the Deming attribution, see Susan Carr, "A Quotation with a Life of Its Own," Patient Safety & Quality Healthcare, Editor's Notebook, July / August 2008, https://www.psqh.com/julaug08/editor.html.

design fits the needs of work at that point in time, but does so no longer.

During the end of the Industrial Revolution, organizations designed systems to manage factories. Most of our current managerial belief system stems from this era in the late 1800s and early 1900s. Frederick Winslow Taylor was the first who formally studied organizations, writing the definitive book on scientific management. He concluded that making people work as hard as they could wasn't as efficient as optimizing the way work was done in systems.

Scientific management systems were created to "optimize" the work. Daily tasks were designed to "crank widgets," to get the work done in as highly efficient and effective ways as possible. Specialization is the order of the day as each worker does one piece of work over and over again. Taylorism is about breaking down work into small, repeatable tasks that can be executed on the large scale. While these systems were big improvements over the ad hoc management and piecemeal craftsmen systems from before, they had their limitations. For example, workers' well-being often wasn't considered important, as they, too, were cogs in the wheel. Leaders who ascribed to Taylorism assumed, as Taylor did, that workers were naturally lazy, and therefore they used strict hierarchies to monitor and control workers closely.

Taylorism carried with it the belief that holding information and knowledge gives someone power. Thinkers designed the work and made all the decisions. The job of the doers, in contrast, was simply to do the work.

Taylorism and scientific management worked well for the Industrial Revolution. At that time, the world didn't change much from one decade to another, so the best predictor of the future was usually the past. A management system molded around certainty and efficiency made sense. Unfortunately, that stable environment no longer exists. That world has been replaced by a rapidly moving and changing Information Age, and we need new systems of management that can keep up.

Mike Arauz, founding member at August, had the following observation that captures this dynamic perfectly: "The difference between optimizing for certainty and optimizing for uncertainty is the core of what separates successful organizations from everyone else" in this new world.[5] So much of the old command-and-control systems aren't serving us. The hard lines between leaders and workers, thinkers and doers, are becoming an active hindrance to success. We need a new way to work.

---

5   Mike Arauz, "The Future of Organizations is Responsive," August, Medium.com, Speaker Notes, February 2016, http://medium.com/21st-century-organizational-development/the-future-of-organizations-is-responsive-5e2e9b5af16a.

A TALE OF TWO ORGANIZATION CHARTS

Let's look at this from another perspective as we compare two org charts, one from the old world and one from the modern workplace.

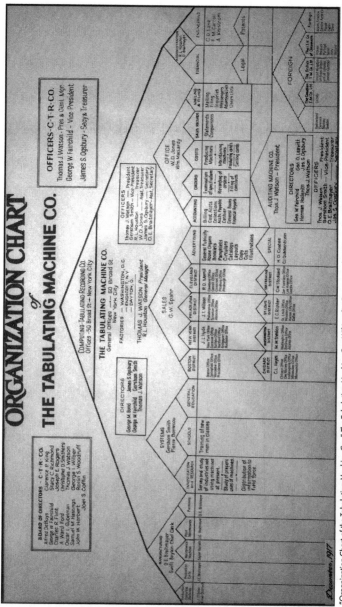

"Organization Chart of the Tabulating Machine Co.," The Tabulating Machine Co., Wikimedia Commons, chart December 1917, picture by Marcin Wichary, https://commons.wikimedia.org/wiki/File:Tabulating_Machine_Co_Organization_Chart.jpg.

This chart originated in 1917 and is from the Tabulating Machine Company, which transitioned into what we know today as IBM.

This second chart is from a modern company. It has a traditional hierarchy and structure, just like the one that the company from the 1920s had. Visually, it looks very similar. There's a pyramid of little boxes connected by lines, just like you saw above.

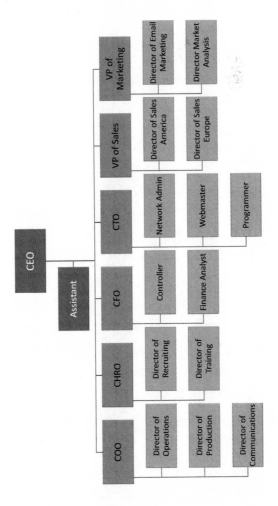

Little else in the modern world looks like it did in the 1920s. Why do our organizations?

A TALE OF TWO BELIEFS

A big part of the reason is due to our outdated beliefs about work. Douglas McGregor explained the basic belief that people are good in his 1960s book *The Human Side of Enterprise*.[6] The idea is that each of us hold one of two beliefs about the motivation and intention of individuals at work. The first is the authoritarian perspective of Theory X. This belief highlights the idea that people are not motivated to work, and management exists to watch and prod individuals to ensure they are being productive and not shirking on the job. Traditional command and control systems inherently hold this belief system, a leftover from the formative years of the Industrial Revolution.

The alternative belief is Theory Y, which assumes people are self-directed and self-motivated in pursuit of shared objectives. With Theory Y, there's an inherent belief people want to do good and work toward a worthy goal without the need for manipulation and coercion. As you might suspect, all of the work in this book rests on the foundation of Theory Y, the belief in the good of humanity and the inherent drive of all individuals to make work a meaningful and fulfilling aspect of their lives.

---

6   Douglas McGregor, *The Human Side of Enterprise* (McGraw-Hill Companies, Inc., 2006).

As we begin to work toward transforming and healing organizations, we must start by examining and shifting our beliefs. Which beliefs serve us and the greater good? Which beliefs can we change or leave behind? As we begin to examine and upgrade our belief systems, we naturally bring in new skills to put those new beliefs into practice. Think about this for yourself. What beliefs can you examine? What new practices could you bring into your leadership to create an environment that people naturally want to be a part of?

For example, whereas we once might have believed leaders need to keep all information private, we now have the opportunity and responsibility to check that belief. Does hoarding information in secrecy make sense? Are the people we work with responsible and able to handle the information in an adult way? If we then decide to share information transparently, we must follow through with new actions and new skills. How can I make this information transparent in a responsible way? What skills will we need in order to take advantage of the benefits of transparency?

As you can see with this brief example, organizations don't change without us as leaders being willing to change, and we can't change without the courage to challenge long-held beliefs and practices. We must become more aware of how we show up in the workplace, examine what we've believed and how we've lived it out—and then have the courage to design it all differently.

Now let's turn our attention to the number one cause of all the things that hold us back—fear.

THE FEAR-BASED WORKPLACE

In traditional organizations, fear is often a quiet, hidden illness that pervades the workplace with toxicity. Fear is to organizations what cancer is to the human system—deadly. We've all experienced it before. Recall the last time you were engaged in a lively work conversation with your colleagues and a high-level boss walked into the room. Suddenly, there was a palpable shift. The conversation either changed completely or the room fell silent. People worried suddenly about what they said and how it might be used against them. Fear appeared in the room like a visitor.

Once, fearful silence was thought of as a good sign for managers. It was thought to be a sign that employees knew their place in the hierarchy and they'd therefore work harder. Today, we know it represents a toxic work environment, one that negatively affects performance and the organization overall.

In traditional organizations, fear feels ever-present.

Employees fear management, afraid to say or do anything apart from the party line for fear they'll lose their job. Managers themselves are in a state of fear, keeping employees in line with harsh and unnecessary rules, policies, and punishments.

All of this fear is a result of the beliefs set in place from the scientific management system of the Industrial Revolution. If we believe that workers are innately lazy, then it's necessary to act with constant oversight, correction, micromanagement, and monitoring. Managers also worry for their own jobs and status in the organization, and fear becomes the lowest common denominator of motivation.

Truth be told, fear is a powerful motivator, but is an even more powerful immobilizer. Once you're no longer in danger or in fear of danger, you're not motivated to take any risks that might lead to the danger again. In addition, fear is inherently self-limiting and can only propel organizations forward so far before it starts pulling them back. Fight or flight is natural when confronting saber-toothed tigers, but in modern organizations, that level of fear radically impairs the ability of individuals, at any organizational level, to function effectively. Fear quickly creates behaviors that eat away at individual productivity and even entire organizations. Instead, what we need is for individuals to feel safe to experiment, to learn from mistakes, to speak up and to voice their opinions. The only way to push fear out is to bring love in.

WHAT ARE THE TOP SIGNS OF A FEAR-BASED WORKPLACE?

1. **Truth:** People are afraid to tell the truth.

2. **Gossip:** The rumor mill is often more credible than official communications.

3. **Public Humiliation:** Managers publicly discredit and shame employees in front of their peers with the intention to send a message to the larger group and improve motivation.

4. **Blame:** There is always someone to blame.

5. **"Yes" Bosses:** People say yes to their bosses because they know that's what gets rewarded, even if it's not what's good for the business.

6. **Appearances:** People become more concerned with how something looks than its results. For example, they might say, "I can't leave until my boss leaves," regardless of the work they actually have to do.

7. **On or Off the Island:** People are constantly talking about who is "in" and who is "out" at the moment—this is an unhealthy preoccupation with status and political capital.

8. **Policy Proliferation:** Policy lists grow immense in size and matter more than common sense.

9. **Secrecy:** Information is hoarded for the sake of power and used to maintain control.

A CRISIS OF ENGAGEMENT

In addition to a fear-based workplace, we have a major crisis of engagement. If you look at recent statistics, the reality is appallingly clear and has not significantly budged in over a decade. According to a Gallup survey, only 13 percent of employees are actually engaged at work. Sixty-three percent are not engaged, and 24 percent are actively disengaged, meaning they're actively looking for ways out. A quarter of all people at work are looking for the door, and over half are apathetic.[7]

You might ask, why does engagement even matter? In simple terms, when people aren't engaged, they aren't as productive. They're not making connections, they're not working at their highest cognitive level, and they're not making the best business decisions. From an organizational perspective, a lack of engagement is extremely harmful. However, even at a personal level, the lack of engagement has serious implications. When you go to work just for a paycheck, you don't feel shared purpose or deeper meaning behind why you do what you do. Your work feels dry and burdensome, and the lack of purpose has massive effects on your overall well-being.

Absenteeism, which is related to disengagement, is also

---

7   Annamarie Mann and Jim Harter, "The Worldwide Employee Engagement Crisis," *Gallup Business Journal*, January 7, 2016, http://news.gallup.com/businessjournal/188033/worldwide-employee-engagement-crisis.aspx.

becoming a significant problem for most organizations. A 2005 study from the US Department of Labor estimated that 3 percent of an employer's workforce is absent on a given day.[8] That might not seem significant, but paid absences cost between 20.9 percent and 22.1 percent of total payroll. Highly engaged business units realize a 41 percent reduction in absenteeism and a 17 percent increase in productivity, according to a Gallup survey, which means that poorly engaged business units are paying for 41 percent more costs in this way.[9] The high price of absenteeism affects organizations even more when lost productivity, morale issues, and labor costs are factored into that equation.

Absenteeism is often misunderstood. It's primarily assessed as a team-level cost or a payroll expense, but that's not the whole story. Sickness and depression happen much more often in difficult work environments, leading to more absenteeism. In a 2000 study by R. Harris at the Bureau of Labor, the author found that heavy workload has no effect on depression; it's the work environment itself and the feeling of being treated unfairly by the management that has the greatest effects on employees' moods. How we treat people in the workplace—and the culture

---

8 "Labor Force Statistics from the Current Population Survey," United States Department of Labor, Bureau of Labor Statistics, accessed April 17, 2018, https://www.bls.gov/cps/cpsaat47.htm.

9 Jim Harter and Annamarie Mann, "The Right Culture: Not Just About Employee Satisfaction," Gallup Business Journal, April 12, 2017, http://news.gallup.com/businessjournal/208487/right-culture-not-employee-happiness.aspx.

we build in our organization—really does matter to the bottom line.

It's time to stop chasing management strategies invented in the Industrial Revolution and forge ahead with new beliefs and practices. We need work and workplaces that are infused with love-based beliefs and practices to create soulful businesses that are good for all those it touches.

This evolutionary path is not easy, but the outcome is desperately needed in the world today. Thankfully, there are leaders and organizations already paving this path and experiencing more caring, engaging, productive, and successful teams and operations. In the chapters ahead, I'll describe the methods they have used to transform their self and their organizations.

CHAPTER TWO

Evolution

FINDING A WAY FORWARD

The act of love is to confront people with their freedom, to assemble, lead in a way that says the choice resides in all of us. What greater gift can we give somebody than the experience of their own power, the experience that they have the capacity to create the world?

—PETER BLOCK[1]

The space between love and fear is vast but also simply a matter of intentional choice. The individual choice to operate from fear or love is one we get to make every day. This small, meaningful choice has great impact on each of us individually and collectively. When we choose fear as leaders, we create isolation and closed channels

---

1   Peter Block, "Servant Leadership."

of communication, as well as a lack of transparency and alignment, which results in people who do not bring their full potential to their role or organization. Put another way, fear leads directly to disengagement, dissatisfaction, and absenteeism in the workplace.

In a love-based organization, in contrast, people feel safe to share information widely, provide open and honest feedback, stretch and grow themselves personally, and pull together for the benefit of the entire organization. Their results and energy are exceptional. How do we move from one to another? This chapter highlights how we find our way forward into a world of work that releases our limiting fears, which have kept us in the shadows of the command-and-control mindset.

The first step in our evolution to the next stage of organizational success is to re-examine our priority on people and culture.

IT'S ALL ABOUT THE PEOPLE

All too often, I hear leaders giving lip service to the importance of people and culture within organizations. Executives often like to say these elements are key priorities, but when the rubber hits the road, almost everything else is prioritized more highly in practice. Additionally, I'll hear the leaders be quick to comment that love and engagement are the "soft stuff"; they claim these are nice-to-have perks that don't impact the overall health of the organization. Studies disagree.

A *Harvard Business Review* article recently reported that employees who felt they worked in a loving, caring culture reported higher levels of satisfaction and teamwork and showed up to work more often. The companies with caring cultures, due in large part to these factors, showed better client outcomes. In healthcare companies, a caring culture led directly to fewer patient trips to the ER, as well as improved mood and quality of life for staff.[2]

According to a Gallup survey, highly engaged business units have employees who are more present and productive, who are more attuned to the needs of customers, and who are more observant of processes, standards, and systems. They achieve a 10 percent increase in customer ratings and a 20 percent increase in sales. With all of these behaviors taken together, highly engaged business units result in 21 percent greater profitability.[3]

A good example of a successful, highly engaged organization is the Netherlands healthcare company Buurtzorg, introduced broadly in Frederic Laloux's book *Reinvent-*

---

2   Sigal Barsade and Olivia A. O'Neill, "Employees Who Feel Love Perform Better," *Harvard Business Review*, January 13, 2014, https://hbr.org/2014/01/employees-who-feel-love-perform-better.

3   Harter and Mann, "The Right Culture."

ing Organizations.[4] This organization has an exemplary human-centered organizational culture and design, which leads them to have less than half the average incidence of sick leave and employee turnover of other home health organizations. Buurtzorg is able to deliver extremely high levels of nurse and patient satisfaction, and extraordinary patient results. Patients required less care, regained autonomy more quickly than average, had fewer emergency hospital admissions, and a shorter length-of-stay after admission. Even more impressively, Buurtzorg's nurses meet patients' needs in far fewer hours than other home healthcare organizations (40 percent of authorized patient care hours compared with an average 70 percent), for far better care at a far lower cost. The company was even able to do all that while maintaining a lower overhead cost than its peers (8 percent of total costs, compared with 25 percent.) Clearly, a culture that cares about its people leads to highly beneficial business outcomes.[5]

Decurion, an organization we'll talk about later in the book, has built a deliberately developmental culture. In essence, they hold a core belief that investing in the development of people means investing in the future of the business. Where some organizations believe that

---

4   Frederic Laloux, *Reinventing Organizations.*

5   B. H. Gray, D. O. Sarnak, and J. S. Burgers, "Home Care by Self-Governing Nursing Teams: The Netherlands' Buurtzorg Model," Commonwealth Fund, May 29, 2015, http://www.commonwealthfund.org/publications/case-studies/2015/may/home-care-nursing-teams-netherlands.

money spent on people takes away from the bottom line, Decurion believes that the two run in concert with one another. Their fantastic business results, they believe, are *because* they invest in their people.

A love-based culture can absolutely garner substantial business advantage, but it is far more important than that in today's world. Emphasizing and embracing love is fundamentally good for the souls of humans. It propels us into a new level of performance and also unleashes our ability to be whole and human at work. We spend almost sixty percent of our waking time at work. Why should that time waste our potential?

READY FOR CHANGE

What got you here, won't get you there.

—MARSHALL GOLDSMITH[6]

We are experiencing sweeping change across the business landscape. Technology is reinventing the way we do business at breakneck speeds, and as a result the speed of change is growing exponentially. The world no longer looks like it did in the Industrial Revolution, and people expect different returns from work than we ever have before. The future will require us to embrace a radical shift

---

6   Marshall Goldsmith, *What Got You Here Won't Get You There: How Successful People Become Even More Successful* (New York: Marshall Goldsmith, 2007), book title.

in how we operate, lead, and design organizations to meet these challenges. To demonstrate the magnitude of the shifts required, here is a graphic that helps differentiate the dramatic organizational shift from the past.

	THEN	NOW
Focus	Profit	Purpose and values
Communication	Secrecy	Transparency
Interaction	Hierarchy	Network of teams
Leadership	Command and control	Servant leader
Strategy	Predict and control	Experiment and iterate
Work style	Competition	Cooperation
Oversight	Micromanaged	Self-managed

How we've operated in the past and what is needed going forward are often in tension. A successful evolving leader must have the capacity to embrace these seemingly contradictory constructs and behaviors and blend them to achieve higher levels of performance, engagement, and success. Profit is still needed as a lifeblood of the organization, but profit without attention to people is no longer sufficient. Teams that are structured and led to respond to this new reality thrive, and others simply do not.

Let me briefly explain the major shifts between the old way and the new.

PROFIT TO PURPOSE

As mentioned previously, organizations have long been focused on the sole pursuit of maximizing shareholder value, but profit is no longer enough. An inspiring and meaningful purpose is proving to bring people together with motivation and passion to achieve the impossible, leading directly to better business results.

SECRECY TO TRANSPARENCY

Gone are the days when information is kept to key individuals at the top of the organization. Information used to connote power and authority, but the silos and barriers ultimately proved to prevent quick and accurate decision-making. Today, successful organizations share information, trusting employees to use the data in productive and effective ways, and pushing decision-making authority to those closest to the issues.

HIERARCHY TO NETWORK OF TEAMS

As the Tale of Two Org Charts showed in Chapter 1, the typical org chart is a relic of the past. A chain of command creates bottlenecks in decision-making, decreased autonomy, and silos that kill integration and innovation. Evolved organizations are adopting alternative structures that leverage highly adaptable, interchangeable, and integrated teams.

COMMAND AND CONTROL TO SERVANT LEADER

The role of a leader is shifting significantly from "managing" to "serving" those around them. The idea that a manager has all the information and knowledge needed to effectively manage and motivate a team (without input from the team themselves) is dying a quick death. This outdated approach wastes essential knowledge and intrinsic motivation within the organization. Today, leaders need to serve and develop contributors on the team all in pursuit of a shared purpose.

PREDICT AND CONTROL TO EXPERIMENT AND ITERATE

We've lost the ability to accurately predict the future. Unfortunately, most traditional organizations still rely on yearly budgeting, forecasting, and five-year strategy exercises, despite the impossibility of their accuracy. Progressive leaders and organizations have long-term vision, but simultaneously rely on real-time data, experiments, and a need to continuously adapt and iterate.

MICROMANAGED TO SELF-MANAGED

Moving into the future of work requires a new level of trust and autonomy that many leaders or managers feel uncomfortable with. Traditional tactics of telling employees what goals to accomplish, what resources to allocate, and which deadlines to complete are being rewritten.

Evolved leaders are acting on the belief that employees are fully competent, trustworthy, responsible adults who can best determine the work that needs to be completed to achieve the shared goals.

Each of these shifts demonstrates the essence of a love-based culture. The practices required to move into them require us to let go of the rampant fear that keeps us in the traditional paradigms, gives freedom and agency back to individuals, and offers genuine care and trust as part of a larger culture of love.

However, there is inherent tension within these shifts. The successful leader will find that thriving in this less predictable environment will require continuous experimentation to find the balance that works for their approach, leadership, and organization.

CHARACTERISTICS OF THE EVOLVED EXECUTIVE

Volumes have been written about the traits of successful leaders. My intent here is not to add to the noise but to highlight the most essential elements for the success of leaders moving into this new paradigm of work. An Evolved Executive leads boldly out of a spirit of soulfulness, humanity, and concern for the greater good. These leaders have a deep passion to continuously expand one's awareness and consciousness to positively impact and serve others. They do not lose track of profit but are rather intentional, testing both the new and old ways against common sense and practice. They embrace the art and science to chart the difficult course into an unknown future. The Evolved Executive starts with the discipline of servant leadership.

SERVANT LEADERSHIP—LOVE IN ACTION

Servant Leadership is a concept first coined for the business world by Robert K. Greenleaf in an essay published in 1970. The basic idea is not difficult—servant leadership is about "serving first." Greenleaf said:

> The difference manifests itself in the care taken by the servant-first to make sure that other people's highest priority needs are being served. The best test, and difficult to administer, is: Do those served grow as persons? Do they, while being served, become healthier, wiser, freer, more autonomous, more likely themselves to become servants? And, what is the effect on the least privileged in society? Will they benefit or at least not be further deprived?

A servant-leader focuses primarily on the growth and well-being of people and the communities to which they belong. While traditional leadership generally involves the accumulation and exercise of power by one at the "top of the pyramid," servant leadership is different. The servant-leader shares power, puts the needs of others first and helps people develop and perform as highly as possible.[7]

The Evolved Executive is one who, instead of focusing on power and control, focuses on the growth and potential of the team in pursuit of the shared vision. There is, however, wide variation on the characteristics of successful servant leaders. The following six traits are most essential to the Evolved Executive and closely align to that of a servant leader.

1. **Authenticity:** the ability and desire to show one's true identity and the willingness to accept our own (and each other's) beautiful brokenness in the journey of learning and growth.

2. **Humility:** an honest understanding of one's strengths and weaknesses, the ability to listen first and ask meaningful questions, the practice of deep appreciation for others, and the ongoing capability to bring out the best in others.

3. **Compassion:** the emotional connection to care for another at work. Compassion is the internal orientation to be other-centered, kind, forgiving and accepting.

---

7   Robert K. Greenleaf, "What is Servant Leadership?" Robert K. Greenleaf Center for Servant Leadership, accessed April 17, 2018, https://www.greenleaf.org/what-is-servant-leadership/.

4. **Expanding Awareness:** engaging in the continuous process of deepening one's self-awareness, consciousness, and personal growth to be in greater service to others.

5. **Accountability:** being able to accept personal responsibility in a collaborative way. To frame work as a way to learn and become individually and collectively responsible.

6. **Courage:** being open to risk and assertively standing up for what one believes is right for the greater good. This can take the form of tough love, as what may be best is not always easy.

These characteristics describe what love looks like in action at work. Love in action does not mean that we're afraid to do hard things, or to confront others with their responsibility. Love in action means we value the wholeness and humanity of others, and we trust and empower them to move their work forward to the betterment of all.

Love in action is human. In traditional organizations, we've lost the ability to take time and simply "be" with people. I like to say we are human "beings" for a reason. Can we stop treating each other as human "doings"? Simple but overlooked genuine questions can make all the difference. How are you? What are you struggling with? What can I do to help? Yes, checking in with others takes time and often gets pushed aside to deal with the next "crisis." However, conversations that connect with people are the most productive conversations we can have. They build trust, provide feedback, and create alignment between individuals and organizations. For an organization in the midst of change, the importance of this practice cannot be overemphasized.

We often forget that each one of us comes into the world with our own agency, our own ability to choose and make an impact on the world around us. Most traditional organizations put enough bureaucracy and policies in place to strip this agency away. Traditional management mindsets quickly tell you what to do, what you can't do, when to show up, where to work, and who to work with. In contrast, organizations and leadership of the future are moving to a place of trust. Each one of us is intelligent, knowledgeable, driven, and can be trusted to be a valuable member of the team. There is work that needs to be done, but how we do it, when we do it, and where we do it is up to us. Working under that kind of trust is an incredibly freeing experience and one that often fosters deep commitment, engagement, and meaning in the work at hand. When workers take ownership of their work, amazing energy and drive emerges.

BUILDING MOTIVATION AND CONNECTION

It should be obvious at this point, but it's worth reiterating: building a love-based culture means caring about people. That not only means watching for opportunities for clear communication, authenticity, and shared decision-making (all important), it also means providing people with what they need to find work motivating and fulfilling.

In his book *Drive*, Dan Pink writes about the three ways we create motivation at work: purpose, autonomy, and mastery. Love in action allows people to bring purpose to their jobs, gives them tools and resources they need to work well, and trusts them to pursue it with autonomy and without constant micromanagement. Love also gives people freedom and responsibility to pursue mastery, true excellence in the skills required by the work. By allowing love to seed the environment with the conditions needed for motivation to grow, we care for our people and create connections with them.

Let's take a minute and address the elephant in the room: we have a deep-seated fear around creating connections with the people who work for us. We have a debilitating belief that says leaders and workers should not get to know one another for a wide variety of reasons. In particular, we are afraid we might have to discipline or even terminate an employee. A relationship with honest human connection might make it harder. This is a damaging, outdated belief. The need for connection, love, and a sense of belonging is part of being human. We all want to be part of something greater than ourselves, loved and connected to those around us in achieving a shared purpose. Neglecting this connection "just in case" means cutting out a core and basic human need, missing out on unrealized potential all for the perceived ease of managing a difficult situation down the road. Again, we see how fear has infiltrated our belief systems. You have a choice to do this differently.

ADULT RELATIONSHIPS AT WORK

Earlier we talked about the belief called Theory X which animates the traditional system; this belief can also be thought of as a patriarchy—a parent-child paradigm. We see the dynamic from managers as well as employees.

> **Managers:** "No matter what I do, I can't get my employees to take initiative, make decisions, have ownership for their work, or manage their own priorities!"

> **Employees:** "If only my boss would let me make my own decisions, let me figure out how to best design this work, stop micromanaging me, and trust me to do my job!"

This dynamic describes the dominant belief system we see in most traditional organizations today. As Peter Block asserts in his book, *Stewardship*, "We already know how to be good parents at work. The alternative, partnership, is something we are just learning about. Our difficulty with creating partnerships is that parenting—and its stronger cousin, patriarchy—is so deeply ingrained in our muscle memory and armature that we don't even realize we are doing it."[8]

In a parent-child relationship, we "protect" our children from situations and information they might not be able to handle. We make decisions for our children. We make our children feel safe by comforting and caretaking, even when our words may not reflect the truth. We see these very same dynamics in the workplace, but in the workplace with adults, these behaviors can be damaging.

We all need to learn how to grow up and be in adult relationships at work. In relationships among adults, we trust others and give others control over their own lives because we believe others can be responsible for their own work and success. We trust adults with information because we know they can handle it. Transparent conversations between adults emphasize freedom and respect, where each of us can make our own decisions and voice our opinions and concerns. Rather than waiting for a boss to tell us what to do, we take responsibility and agency for our own impact at work, which is a far more fulfilling way to work.

---

8   Peter Block, *Stewardship: Choosing Service Over Self Interest* (Oakland: Berrett-Koehler Publishers, 1993), 16.

FACING OTHER FEARS

Moving into a love-based culture can feel terrifying on several levels. Command-and-control bureaucracies are often based in the scarcity model, which says there are never enough resources, time, money, or talent, and too much competition. The idea of allowing for more freedom at work is often at odds with the model. Freedom, similar to abundance, says that there's always enough and that we're moving in the direction we need to be moving. Moving to this evolved level requires we let go of a fear of scarcity and embrace abundance and freedom.

Within this fear hides an often deeper resistance—the fear of truly being seen. Meaningful change requires us to step into our own authority, drive our own work, and speak up for what we believe is right. Oftentimes, that results in vulnerability. It's only natural to feel anxious about looking incompetent, or being embarrassed in front of our colleagues. Yet, these fears lead us to keep our mouths shut—to keep the status quo. To reach a culture of love, we must be bold. We must break out of the self we developed to survive in the old hierarchy. We must tap into our own mastery and shift the way we know ourselves at work.

Changing the dynamic is difficult and requires that we each individually face our own fears. As you'll find as we move through the following chapters of this book, it's only by facing our fears, becoming more self-aware, and choosing new beliefs and practices that we will be able to evolve and lead organizations into the future.

THE TIME IS NOW

Change can be hard. However, with any kind of evolution, we have the inspiring opportunity to create a new and better way of being. When we're in the messy middle of change, it's hard to see the forest for the trees. We know the old way isn't working, we see the suffering at work, but it's hard to understand what the new way will be like.

Even though the path forward feels unclear and challenging, the journey will be worth the difficulty. Organizations are already thriving on the other side, taking in data from the environment, becoming nimbler in how they work. Individuals are finding deeper meaning and fulfillment as they operate from their whole selves and take responsibility for the success of their work. As organizations release fear and the chain of command, work becomes more efficient, effective, purposeful, and meaningful.

What is at stake is your future, and the future of work for your children and grandchildren. What kind of workplace do you want to spend your days building? What are you willing to do to make it happen?

It all starts with *you*.

PART II

Begin from Within

CHAPTER THREE

Leadership Beliefs and Consciousness

Like a computer's operating system, our beliefs underlie everything we do, whether we consciously realize it or not. As we become changemakers in our own lives, teams, and organizations, the first step is the least obvious. We must ensure that the beliefs we hold, the values that underpin our mental operating system, are aligned with the future we want to create.

Creating a new self with new beliefs is much more challenging than most realize. Changing beliefs requires incredible awareness, discipline, and desire. As Joe Dispenza says in *You Are the Placebo*, "We're addicted to our beliefs; we're addicted to the emotions of our past... We've in fact conditioned ourselves to believe all sorts of things that aren't necessarily true—and many of these things are having a negative impact on our health and happiness."[1]

When we default to unconscious beliefs based on fear, these beliefs sharply limit our natural abilities and effectiveness. A belief system based on fear will emphasize behaviors around hoarding information, isolating and controlling others, and using knowledge as power. It will lead to the very kinds of dysfunction and disengagement we are confronted with in today's traditional organizations—the Fortune 500 Disease and crisis of suffering. In contrast, beliefs based on love in action emphasize behaviors that lead to transparency, openness, and inclusion in decision-making. An honest belief in the good of humankind naturally leads to empowered, engaged colleagues.

Due to the difficulty in understanding and seeing our beliefs, we often move toward superficial attempts at change by addressing only the behavioral level. I have been on a deep journey of self-awareness and personal development over the past ten years, working with a variety of deeply talented practitioners and coaches on the behavioral level. I achieved marginal change at best until I began befriending and dismantling my belief system. Only then did change happen quickly. When we neglect underlying beliefs, we neglect the root cause of why we

---

1   Joe Dispenza, *You Are the Placebo: Making Your Mind Matter* (Carlsbad, California: Hay House, 2014), 166.

act the way we do. Adding new or different behaviors and skills allows individuals the opportunity to change tactics in the short term but does not connect to the reasons why we act and, thus, is often ultimately ineffective. Belief drives behavior.

In my coaching practice, I hunt for limiting beliefs that stand in the way of the outcomes my clients want to see. For example, maybe you say yes to work all the time, and you can't say no even when you know you should. We can work on the behavior; we can practice saying no. For most people, practicing behavior leads to mediocre short-term adjustments. No matter how hard they work initially, in the long term, most people will resort back to prior habits because those habits are aligned with their deeper beliefs. If one of your core beliefs tells you that the only way to feel valued at work is to say yes to any assignment, saying no only creates internal conflict for you. Thus, saying no will continue to hurt every time you do it until the underlying belief is changed or resolved.

Let's try a thought experiment. Think of one behavior you do regularly that you'd like to change. Spend a moment to think about why you do this behavior—fill in the blank to the following sentence.

I [insert behavior] so that I don't have to [insert outcome].

Example: I [say yes to work I cannot complete] so that I don't have to [disappoint others, create conflict, or look like I can't handle the work].

Can you see how, in this example, the behavior exists to relieve you from feeling a certain way? Every belief exists because it provides you a benefit. To create long-lasting change, you have to examine what belief is motivating your behavior and decide if the belief, in fact, serves your greatest good. (Probably, it isn't, and you'll need to replace that belief with one that does.)

The same is true when you attempt to create change in organizations. Creating change as a leader is like attempting to turn a very large ship in a short amount of time. To do so effectively, you need to become keenly aware of the underlying belief systems in yourself and in the organization that may be in conflict with the change you'd like to implement. Most leaders try to implement change in a very surface way, checking boxes to complete the activities on an outdated change management plan. They use a "talking at you" approach with their people, sending down lists of actions with the message that we "have to do this." Unfortunately, simply addressing a "burning platform" or "communicating the change" will almost never lead to successful evolution. It's far more effective to dive deep into underlying belief systems, and to work with your people collaboratively, to cocreate the change together. Doing so requires that you be willing to have deep and sometimes uncomfortable conversations, that you invite others into the discussion of competing priorities, and that you ask for solutions at the front lines. By framing change as something we all do together, all the time, starting with beliefs, you are able to create a lasting evolution that meets the true needs of the organization.

BEGIN WITH SELF-AWARENESS

How do we tackle our limiting beliefs? It all starts with self-awareness, something author Tasha Eurich identifies as the most critical metaskill of the twenty-first century.[2] Self-awareness cultivates an honest inventory of how we see ourselves, how others see us, and who we really are. This is sorely needed in today's world of work. After all, we've all seen how "the least competent people are usually the most confident in their abilities."[3] The lack of self-awareness can have devastating effects on team performance, morale, and organizational effectiveness. Furthermore, studies have shown clearly that a lack of self-awareness is a nontrivial business problem. Senior executives who lack this ability are 600 percent more likely to derail, costing companies as much as a staggering $50 million per executive.[4]

---

2   Dr. Tasha Eurich, *Insights: the Surprising Truth About How Others See Us, How We See Ourselves, and Why the Answers Matter More Than We Think* (reprint, New York: Random House, 2017/2018), 8.

3   Eurich, *Insights*, 14.

4   Eurich, *Insights*, 12.

Fostering self-awareness requires that we reflect on our actions and ask ourselves difficult questions on an ongoing basis. For example: Why did I get so upset at Joe in today's meeting? What about my actions created the situation? How do others perceive me and my abilities? What are my actions telling others? Oftentimes when we ask hard questions of ourselves, we find we don't like the answers. This is a good sign and provides one of the most powerful catalysts for change. Until we inquire more deeply and see things from a different perspective, it is nearly impossible to effect change. Be grateful for these moments of painful recognition as they are setting you up for personal growth.

Deepening your self-awareness has huge payoffs. It leads to a keen understanding of your belief system and makes change possible, and it makes you a more present and effective leader. That being said, the process also carries a burden. Growing into a new way of being and doing can make you show up differently at work, which can challenge relationships. People may say, "Well, that's not the Sarah I know. Sarah used to be so quiet and reserved and would always take on extra work. Now, she's telling me no and speaking out about her frustration in meetings." Be prepared that awareness, and the change that results, will be challenging for both you and others.

HORIZONTAL AND VERTICAL LEARNING

Recent studies on leadership development strategies point to two distinct types of learning and growth for leaders in progressive organizations—what we will call the horizontal and vertical.

Horizontal learning focuses on the information, skills, and competencies we need to succeed as leaders in organizations. It's essential for clearly defined problems. Vertical learning, in contrast, adds to what I call "heart intelligence," or emotional intelligence. It is the ability to interpret a complex situation or data in meaningful ways based on our beliefs. Vertical learning is essential to being able to address complex adaptive problems, tough relationships, and rapidly changing circumstances.

In my own practice, I think of these complementary pathways as head knowledge (horizontal) and heart intelligence (vertical). Head knowledge is what you know: technical expertise, functional skills, and behaviors. Heart intelligence focuses on developing our emotional intelligence, as well as upgrading our leadership operating system to be more wise, intelligent, intuitive, and caring.

Horizontal and vertical knowledge are complementary and work best in concert with one another. To have one without the other is to sharply limit a leader's success. In today's world of work, we are good at identifying and learning in this horizontal area of skill development. Leaders become leaders by building strong horizontal competence in their fields, so they are naturally attuned to this dimension of learning. Where we need intense focus and work in the modern era of rapid change is instead in our vertical knowledge. Vertical knowledge stems from self-awareness and is far more critical to our desired path of Evolved Executives in modern organizations.

Vertical learning first begins with our understanding of consciousness. We live in a world of constant and exponential change. The trick is to see our own beliefs, how we view the world and how our assumptions, behaviors, and attitudes affect the world around us. By doing so, we are able to see *how* things change, and to make intentional decisions to take advantage of opportunities rather than being confused or overwhelmed by them. By expanding our awareness, we increase our consciousness—an essential component to vertical learning.

THE APARTMENT BUILDING

I love Caroline Myss's teaching on the topic of consciousness. Myss uses the analogy of an apartment building to describe a very powerful lesson about developing our own consciousness and the astonishing blessings and struggles that come with the climb. The following section is taken from her video teachings. Caroline explains,

Consciousness is like an apartment building with many floors. People have different views of the world, depending on which floor they occupy. You may have an ocean view on the tenth floor, but your neighbors on the first floor say they don't live near the ocean because they only see the parking lot. In a similar way, inside ourselves, we all have these floors of consciousness and perception. Every time we move up a floor, the world around us changes. We see the landscape differently.

However, there's a price to moving up. Just as rent gets higher as you move up in a luxury apartment building, moving up in this building has added expense—you pay with alienation from your neighbors and colleagues. The higher you move up in the building, the less your neighbors want to hear about what you see. Just imagine your upstairs neighbor visits you and excitedly tells you about the gorgeous sunsets and snow-capped mountain ranges in the distance. All the while, you're on the third floor and all you can see is an overgrown park, the next building over, a few streets, and your neighbors entering and exiting the building. Mostly you smell the dumpsters outside your window. You'll tell your neighbor, "Go back to your penthouse suite and don't let the door smack you on your way up." Most people don't want to question everything they know and hold dear.

Alienation from others isn't the only price to pay as you climb the building. With every floor you go up, there's a new expense. You must reevaluate your beliefs and values. You must face difficult questions about the meaning and purpose of your life that you've never explored before. You must face the pressure, the doubt, and ridicule of others who resent your new ideas. The price adds up.

However, as you rise, new skills and abilities begin to flourish. The physical senses that were so prominent and useful for you on the first floor begin to expand as you rise in your building. Seeing shifts to perceiving. Hearing shifts to sensing. The new senses don't override your physical senses, rather working together in harmony.[5]

These new inner insights become a tremendous asset for you in understanding the world around you on a deeper level. I know the inner insights have ignited a profound transformation in my own life and experience. Can I predict the future with my sensing abilities? No. However, I

---

[5]   Myss talks about this teaching in nearly every workshop and webinar she does. This particular explanation is a compilation of her teachings from the following: Caroline Myss, "Spiritual Direction: Pebbles in the Well-Learning to Listen to Your Soul—2015," video, 1:37:33, accessed May 16, 2018, https://www.youtube.com/watch?v=EEnHo1sTEo0; Caroline Myss, "Going Deep: Using Archetypes to Explore Personal and Global Change—2014," video, 10:17, accessed May 16, 2018, https://www.youtube.com/watch?v=C3RLPYgActI; Caroline Myss, "Healing: A Mystical Science That Includes Miracles—Dublin 2014," video, 1:26:54, accessed May 16, 2018, https://www.youtube.com/watch?v=9Pwj401H58U.

have a depth of inner knowing and guidance I've never experienced before. I'm overwhelmed with gratitude for this knowledge, and yet I feel keenly the price I've paid for it.

The fact of the matter is we all start on the first floor. We see the world as we want to see it. We all find the staircase, and we know the world around us is going to change. Those of us who climb the stairs have the drive to face the fear, embrace the unknown, and experience the new levels. We are willing to pay the price to see the bigger world.

The journey can be overwhelming and scary. As you progress, you'll find you need to adjust, deciding all over again what is true. For me, each move has led to a deep questioning, with the fear that nothing may hold true any longer. The disorienting fearfulness that results from every stage is one of the hardest things I've ever faced in my life. The reward on the other side, however, is peace, love, joy, and meaning. I share this analogy to set a foundation for us to build upon throughout the remainder of the book. Fear is a normal part of this process. What lies on the other side is the possibility and potential for a more purposeful and meaningful existence.

The world needs leaders who can embrace this fear and continue to upgrade their senses, beliefs, and vision—their vertical knowledge or heart's intelligence. We need to heal and to have the courage to build purposeful, adaptable, innovative, and thriving teams and organizations. The cost of staying the same is far too great. As Robert Frost so eloquently stated, "The best way out is always through."[6] We must go through this messy middle of change.

DEVELOPING OUR CONSCIOUSNESS

When you begin to develop your heart's intelligence, your levels of consciousness and vertical learning, you expand your awareness, which leads to increased leadership abilities. In fact, research at the National Security Agency finds that "executive mindset failure is one of the biggest drivers for why executives fail" and "most leaders are hitting a mental and emotional glass ceiling, unable to effectively navigate today's business environments."[7] Increasing our levels of consciousness may, in fact, be the secret ingredient to leadership and organizational success going forward.

Vertical learning and development of consciousness are intimately related. Harvard professor Robert Kegan says, "Vertical learning catalyzes a quantum increase in mental complexity, which radically improves a leader's ability to

---

6   Robert Frost, *North of Boston* (New York City: Henry Holt and Company, 1915), 31.

7   Barrett C. Brown, "The Future of Leadership for Conscious Capitalism," MetaIntegral Associates white paper, accessed April 24, 2018, http://integral-life-home.s3.amazonaws.com/ MetaIntegral-Brown-TheFutureOfLeadershipForConsciousCapitalism.pdf, 3.

navigate today's highly complex, ambiguous, and rapidly changing context and cascades those new skills into the entire organization."[8]

Based on over forty years of research, management scientist Bill Tolbert developed a model that includes several distinct levels of vertical learning. This model is critical to how I came to the idea of the Evolved Executive. He shared this model in a *Harvard Business Review* article called "Seven Transformations of Leadership."

Just as human development goes through a series of phases, so does leadership development. As we grow through these levels of development, just like moving up floors in the apartment building, we experience an increase in mental and emotional capabilities. Interestingly, Brown from MetaIntegral Associates, found that 85 percent of the leaders in the West fit within one of the first four levels of development with the fifth level growing the most rapidly. Right now, only 5 percent of leaders are in the upper levels 6 through 8. These are the most likely of all leaders to "reliably generate organizational transformation."[9]

There are deeply significant organizational advantages for operating at higher levels of development. For exam-

8   Brown, "The Future of Leadership," 2.

9   Brown, "The Future of Leadership," 3.

ple, Brown's research found that "leaders who develop themselves into the later levels [6 through 8] have access to enhanced and highly-attuned mental, emotional, and relational capacities that others don't. They are able to act with greater wisdom and deeper care than ever before... [and strengthen] their ability to effectively respond to the complex, ambiguous, and sophisticated challenges of the 21st century leadership."[10]

As a leader moves from the lower levels to the higher ones, I would argue that he or she moves from leading from fear to leading from love. He or she begins to shift core beliefs and practices from fear (self-protection, power status, rules and policies) to practices focused on love (organizational and personal growth/transformation, self-fulfillment, self-awareness, greater good, vision, and purpose).

There's nothing inherently better or worse about being at higher levels of development. A toddler is not inherently better than a teenager, even though the teenager can do more complex and demanding tasks. Higher levels are not for everyone; there is a price to pay for every level, and all levels have value. As we move to higher levels, we can think and act in more sophisticated ways to face more complex challenges. When we run into the limits of the levels we are on, we choose to embrace growth. The work

10   Brown, "The Future of Leadership," 8.

I do focuses on leaders who want to move on to higher levels because it's important to them, not because some expert says they need to in order to be of more value to the organization.

In the business world, we've gotten really good at horizontal development; we're good at understanding competencies and skills as the mental components needed to move an organization forward. To move into levels that can handle the new, rapidly changing world, however, we must be willing to do the work to dive into this vertical space. We must be willing to go to higher levels to tap into other sources of intellect—not just using our brains, but opening our hearts to deeper levels of emotional intelligence, and opening our senses to dynamics in our environments, teams, and cultures.

Expanding to these higher levels is an intensely personal journey, but it has immediate impact on our ability to create positive transformations in the organizations we lead. Expansion allows for greater creativity and freedom. It allows us to tap into a greater potential within each of us—and within our organizations at large. It allows us to act with more integrity and authenticity.

There is no turning back once you have reached a new level of growth. I like to say, "You can't un-know this stuff." You can't pretend you don't know. Your new awareness might lead to the realization that you're not "a good fit" for a role anymore or that your life purpose, or your organization's purpose, is different than what you believed. Clarity becomes an obvious and powerful motivator in your life.

If you can embrace the cost of growth, reaching new vertical levels gives you freedom and information to make different choices. It gives you greater ability to act and design your life according to your soul's purpose.

HOW DOES VERTICAL GROWTH COME ABOUT?

I've come to realize that significant growth arrives unexpectedly, most often as a result of a crisis. Two prerequisites have to be in place. One, there is a general sense that something's not right (that nagging feeling I described in my own personal story). Maybe how you've led or managed in the past isn't working anymore. You might be frustrated or concerned that people are disengaged, not taking ownership when you think they should. You're putting in more and more effort simply to feel more burnt out doing what you think needs to be done. Something is just not right. You know there has got to be a better way.

For example, most organizations ask managers and leaders to forecast sales targets for the end of the year at the beginning of the year. We know the spreadsheet will inevitably be useless by the time the fourth quarter comes around, but it's what management wants us to do. The frustration, and the soul-sucking requirements of the job, make you think, "There's got to be a better way."

The second prerequisite for significant vertical growth is a deep desire to become more self-aware. Whereas the first prerequisite is a dissatisfaction with the way things are, the second is a curiosity and willingness to do the work. You recognize that you're part of the problem, and so you accept that you must be part of the solution. You're willing to do the work both organizationally and personally to make a difference.

Getting to the place where you're willing to face the problem and to do the work often results from a life crisis. Brené Brown talks about going through a mental breakdown. She worked on what she thought was going to be a short research project on shame. It became an extended inquiry that led her to a point of questioning everything she believed to be true. While her therapist called that a spiritual awakening, Brené says, "It felt like a textbook breakdown."[11] Leaders often go through something similar as they move from traditional ways of leading from fear to a place of evolution, leading from love. The crisis can be a very specific experience, like getting fired from

---

11 Brené Brown, *The Gift of Imperfection: Let Go of Who You Think You're Supposed to Be and Embrace Who You Are* (Center City, MN: Hazelden, 2010), xii.

a job. Or it can be more of a quiet revolution within you, where you become more and more burnt out over a year, knowing you need something different because the joy has drained out of your life.

A crisis alone is not enough, however. In every crisis there's a crux point, where the world gets narrow and scary. A lot of times, people choose not to move through the worst point because it requires so much courage and difficult inner work. Those that walk through, however, come out the other side wholly different. The research that came out of Brené's crisis became a TED Talk and the book that catalyzed her career. I assume she never could have imagined the end result in the middle of the struggle.

Oftentimes, we *have* to crack to be willing to move through that crux point. I have cracked myself. So much of me was burnt out, I felt like I would split in two. I could no longer go forward in the way I knew how, and so I walked through the hardship.

Moving into deeper levels of consciousness around leadership takes a journey far less traveled, because it requires the difficult inner work in that crux point. We have to face our own judgements, cynicisms, and fears, which is not easy or fun. We put all the beliefs we have held in our lives on the table and test them to see if they're still true today. Some people find it to be exciting and freeing to let go of beliefs that have held them back. Others find it scary and anxiety-provoking.

As you face this journey, ask yourself: how intensely do you want to grow? How much do you need to develop in your awareness of yourself and others in order to spark meaningful change? Once you face the crux point, you might come out knowing you need to leave your job or completely change how you're leading the organization. You might have to change everything you know, and you must be ready.

Most clients who come to me are ready; they realize they've gotten as far as they can on their own, and need help to get further along. They're motivated to move through the crux point and into the greater awareness and greater freedom of the other side. They're ready to do the work.

BREAKING THE HABIT

As Dr. Joe Dispenza says, "If you want a new outcome, you have to break the habit of being yourself, and reinvent a new self."[12] I believe that's true as it relates to leaders and organizations as well. If we want to create something new, we have to break the habits of our old way of being.

---

12   Dr. Joe Dispenza, *Breaking the Habit of Being Yourself: How to Lose your Mind and Create a New One* (Carlsbad, CA: Hay House, 2012), 22.

It's taken years to get where we are today. The beliefs and habits I have today have grown over decades, and they won't change overnight. Old habits are so ingrained and programmed in our ways of being that it requires real effort to, as Dispenza says, break the habit of being yourself to become a new self. It's a one-day-at-a-time, constant iteration of change. Every day we grow a little, test ourselves, and challenge ourselves all over again to be the greatest version of ourselves possible today. It's not a quick fix.

THE UPSIDE

While the journey is long and hard, the destination is incredible. The clarity and freedom that results from this process gives you the ability to navigate more complexity in your world. You have greater access to more kinds of intelligence. Speaking for myself, there's a greater sense of meaning and clarity around my purpose. I have a greater sense of direction around how I make decisions that guide my life, and a different level of commitment in pursuit of my goals. When what I'm trying to achieve feels sacred, I'm willing to do whatever it takes.

I know that, today, my purpose is to awaken the souls of leaders so we can create soulful organizations. I have full-on commitment. If something aligns with my purpose, I'm a full-body yes. If it only halfway aligns, I'm a no. It's a much different level of commitment, confirmation, and affirmation around what I'm doing and why I'm doing it.

It's easy to be paralyzed when you don't know what you want to do and how you want to show up in this world. When we get out of our heads and are able to be in our wholeness, aligned with our mind, body, and soul, we become much more attuned to what it is we're supposed to be doing here in the world. We act decisively, without waffling, and we get exponentially better results.

There is clear benefit for our organizations as well. The suffering at work—evident in huge levels of disengagement, absenteeism, and frustration—makes it clear that now is the time to change. Most people have a constant feeling of "I just have to go get a paycheck" rather than a feeling of excitement about what they do.

It's time to end the suffering. Work can be a place where we find fulfillment and meaning, a "pilgrimage of our identity," as David Whyte calls it.[13] I've seen it happen! There's so much potential in all of us to be a powerful source of good, but at this point, leaders and organizations are unprepared to realize that potential.

We need a massive shift. We need people who are willing

---

13   David Whyte, *Crossing the Unknown Sea: Work as a Pilgrimage of Identity* (New York: Riverhead Books, 2002), title.

to pay the price of moving into new levels of awareness and clarity, people who are willing to do the work to transform themselves and their organizations with love in action—we need Evolved Executives. I believe that you can be one of them.

CHAPTER FOUR

Developing Evolutionary Beliefs

I've worked with many leaders and teams over the last ten years and have noticed several patterns. As leaders move to greater levels of awareness and effectiveness, a few evolutionary mindsets tend to surface over and over again. These are the healthy, vibrant beliefs I'll talk about in the next pages. As you journey toward higher levels of development and leadership, use these as a starting point, a shortcut for your journey ahead.

Also keep in mind the need for traditional skills—the horizontal growth detailed in Chapter 3. The beliefs and mindsets referred to here balance *how* you know with more refined ways of being that lead you into the future. As you grow into these beliefs and begin putting them into action, you'll need to refine your horizontal skills as well.

Most leaders are already exceptionally skilled in the horizontal areas—the analytical thinking required to be good managers and the day-to-day skills of business—but they need assistance to gain insight with the heart and the will. The heart accesses emotional intelligence, knowledge of people, and sensing the environments around you. The will, when accessed deliberately, can heighten your ability to connect with your authentic purpose and fulfill that purpose through action. The following beliefs will help you connect with both.

CRITICAL BELIEFS

Let's begin with four critical leadership beliefs: the connection mindset, the growth mindset, the trust mindset, and the all-important purpose mindset.

As you read about these beliefs, spend time checking in with your reaction to each. Do you have resistance to a belief? Relief? Questions? This list is most helpful when it informs your personal journey. What would it take for you to believe or embrace each belief?

THE CONNECTION MINDSET

Connection is a basic human need in all of us. What we get at work so often instead is disconnection—survival of the fittest, each man or woman for his- or herself, backstabbing, and throwing each other under the bus. To move forward, we need to question why we insist on the fear-driven, individualistic beliefs that lead to disconnection. How can we let go of the fear and instead begin to meet our need for human connection?

Scientist Matthew Lieberman wrote a great book called *Social: Why Our Brains Are Wired to Connect*. He says our need for connection is as foundational as our need for food and water.[1] At work, we often forget we are human with human needs. We try to shut off our need for connection as we walk in the door, putting on a heart shield so we won't let anyone get to us or hurt us. We try to shut off part of ourselves, but in so doing, we starve our souls of connection and belonging.

One of my favorite authors, Margaret Wheatley, says, "You can't hate someone whose story you know."[2] This gets to the heart of some of our issues at work. We tell our leaders not to get to know their teams too deeply for fear they might have to discipline or terminate them. As I've said

---

1 Matthew D. Lieberman, *Social: Why Our Brains Are Wired to Connect* (New York: Crown Publishing, 2013).

2 Margaret J. Wheatley, *Turning to One Another* (San Francisco: Berrett-Koehler, 2009), 95.

before, this is shortsighted. In fact, in my own research, I've found that one of the greatest levers of engagement is "feeling valued" at work. Feeling valued can be described as feeling a manager cares about me as a person, knows what is important to me, and recognizes my contributions. It is human and beneficial to know another's story.

We discussed earlier how important it is for organizations to emerge from the mechanistic Industrial Era mindset. In this mindset, employees are like cogs in the wheel of the organizational machine, but that's not enough in today's world. Individuals are now looking for much more than a simple paycheck. We look for human connection and belonging. This connection and belonging has been described as "emotional currency" or even "psychic income."[3] We are looking for an environment that pays in this currency, fulfilling our emotional and social needs in addition to our financial needs. In short, we want to work for a leader and an organization that is psychologically rewarding. We long to change the mechanistic relationship of alienation to a relationship that instead celebrates connection and creates health. The more open and genuine you can be with your colleagues, the more you understand where they're coming from, the more you can lead with love even in the face of a difficult conversation or situation.

---

3   Rajendra Sisodia, Jagdish N. Sheth, and David Wolfe, *Firms of Endearment: How World-Class Companies Profit from Passion and Purpose*, 2nd ed. (Indianapolis: Pearson FT Press, 2014), 107.

Think about it. If you were about to be disciplined or terminated, would you rather have it be with someone who genuinely cares about you and knows your story? Or would you prefer this conversation with someone who lacks any human connection and doesn't really care? Coldness is not the way we are designed to treat one another. People think that distance will avoid litigation, but that also is misguided. Even in the healthcare field, there is research that says physicians who are more open with their patients about errors are less likely to get sued.[4]

True Belonging

Brené Brown recently wrote a book called *Braving the Wilderness*, in which she describes a crisis of disconnection in our society. We've basically sorted ourselves into small groups, turned away from one another, and moved instead toward blame. Brown would say we've gotten to this place due to our fear of vulnerability, criticism, and failure. The solution is what she calls true belonging, which she defines as, "a spiritual practice of believing and belonging to yourself so deeply that you can share your authentic self with the world... True belonging does not require you to change who you are. It requires you to be who you are."[5]

---

4   Aaron E. Carroll, "To Be Sued Less, Doctors Should Consider Talking to Patients More," *The New York Times*, June 1, 2015, https://www.nytimes.com/2015/06/02/upshot/to-be-sued-less-doctors-should-talk-to-patients-more.html.

5   Brené Brown, *Braving the Wilderness: The Quest for True Belonging and the Courage to Stand Alone* (New York: Random House, 2017), 38.

Brown says that only once we believe thoroughly in our-selves can we truly belong. True belonging only happens when we present our authentic, imperfect self to the world. Our sense of belonging can never be greater than our sense of self-acceptance.[6] At the core of human belonging is acceptance of yourself in all your glory—the good, bad, and ugly. When you are able to do that, you can open up new realms of connection for others.

Acceptance of self begins with love, with letting go of fear. We all fear being seen as broken, less than, or imperfect, but love says it's okay to be exactly how you show up in the world. When you truly love and accept yourself, that love allows others to show up authentically. It lets them know you will accept them as part of the tribe regardless.

Belonging does not come at the cost of our authenticity, freedom, or power. You have a greater sense of power when you're acting from your authentic self. When you show up how others feel like you should show up, you restrict much of your power and creativity because you're constrained in a box. Being able to show up as your whole self with the freedom of your own creativity, discretion, and agency has beautiful ramifications for both the individual and the organization. The individual is able to realize their full potential, while the organization is able

6   Brown, *Braving the Wilderness*, 30.

to tap into their incredible creativity, innovation, drive, and motivation.

When we as leaders model wholeness and imperfection, we create a sense of connection with others. To do this, we must be willing to step into a place of vulnerability, to embrace our fears and let others know when we are uncertain or when we don't have the answers. We must be willing to admit to our shortcomings, to ask for help when we need it, and to accept our limitations. This courageous vulnerability gives those around the leader a chance to say, "Wow, that was pretty impressive," and then allow their own vulnerabilities to show as well. In contrast, when someone shows up very guarded, impersonal, or is in it only for themselves, they create an environment that reflects those traits. We all want to be part of something bigger than ourselves. True belonging and purpose allow us to be part of something bigger only when leaders have the courage to lead from vulnerability.

To achieve true belonging at work, we must challenge the beliefs that drive disconnection, separation, the "in-" or "out-crowd" effect, and have the courage to model connection and love. Organizations that are soulful, purpose driven, and humanistic begin with leaders modeling the same values on an individual level. How can you operate more in authenticity, human connection, and true belonging? How can you invite others to be part of something bigger than themselves?

GROWTH MINDSET

When we talk about the mindsets or belief systems that lead to healthy, vibrant organizations, the second critical mindset is valuing growth rather than the status quo. So often in society and the corporate world we have a mindset that we don't or can't change, that our values and belief systems were solidified at a young age, so then we should just deal with the cards we're dealt. Nothing could be further from the truth, and this outdated belief cripples growth.

People can change, and we evolve naturally all the time. It is true, however, that people don't like to *be changed*. I hear over and over, "We need to change them. He or she needs to do this differently—now." Forcing people to do anything with a threat to their job or punitive steps will have limited long-term effect. No one likes to have change forced upon them. However, engagement and fulfillment rise significantly when employees are involved in the changes affecting their lives. I've seen massive results when people make the conscious decision to create and embrace change themselves.

Dr. Carol Dweck coined the terms "growth mindset" and "fixed mindset" in her book *Mindset*[7] after doing research involving thousands of children and the impact of their mindsets on their outcomes. If you have a fixed mindset,

7   Dr. Carol Dweck, *Mindset: The New Psychology of Success* (New York: Random House, 2006).

you believe qualities like intelligence or talent are fixed traits that cannot be changed. You also believe talent alone creates your success without additional effort—creating an unfortunate need to constantly prove yourself. You believe your performance proves (or disproves) your worth. You ask, "Will I look smart or dumb? Will I be accepted or rejected?"[8]

With a growth mindset, you believe "that your basic qualities are things you can cultivate through your efforts, your strategies, and help from others."[9] These most basic abilities can be developed through dedication and hard work over time, and your brains, intellect, and talent are just the starting point. This creates a love of learning and a resilience essential for great accomplishments and great leadership. If your performance on this task doesn't reflect on your worth, you are free to fail and to learn from that failure in useful ways. Many of the exemplary leaders we see in organizations today have this perspective.

Society does value intelligence and personality, and it's normal to desire these traits and to show them to the world, but believing these attributes are fixed only limits our success. By embracing a growth mindset, and the learning and persistence that come with that mindset, we are free to get better over time. If we can change and grow our

8   Dweck, *Mindset*, 14.

9   Dweck, *Mindset*, 14.

intelligence and personality through actual experience, we are not set in stone. Who we are and where we can go in our lives is determined, then, by what we learn along the way and what we *do* with that learning.

Why do we waste time proving over and over again how great we are rather than focusing on getting better? Why do we look for people who make us feel comfortable versus those who will make us stretch? Why do we seek out the status quo versus looking for better ways of solving the problems we face?

The unsurprising answer is fear.

My Journey with Fear

The idea that we can change and always do change has been paramount to my own growth. However, it has not come without a healthy dose of fear.

As a coach, I work a lot with fear. With my clients, we work to understand and overcome fears, limiting beliefs, and behaviors that hold us back, the lies that make us stop growing, taking risks, and showing up fully. To be the coach I want and need to be, I also must do constant work on myself. I must be able to see and face my own fears, to get to know them and where they came from, and to offer them a chance to move on.

If I am truly and deeply honest with myself, fear is ever present. It's my shadow, following me always. As a Midwest kid who grew up with a fixed mindset, fear was my biggest motivator, though it also limited and paralyzed me at times, as it does everyone. Even now, if I am not present and conscious in how I interact with the world, I feel fear. It sneaks up on me, making me feel like an imposter or telling me not to put my whole self out for the world to see and criticize. However, today I am much better at seeing the fear and asking her to step aside to allow room for my natural state of love to fill me.

Writing this book is a perfect example. It's been a continuous process of facing my fears, and I've had to lean in every time. If I let my fears control me, I would never have finished this book. I might have pointed the finger at someone, anyone else, and said that the process of writing has been stressful, and has not allowed my true voice and true skills to come to light. At the end of the day, though, it would have been my own fears that were stopping me. Being able to share my perspective with the world, helping other leaders in organizations move along this path is what keeps me going. There was a point in my life when I would have stopped, but I know now that facing fears for what they are is what propels us forward.

Ask yourself, when do you feel fear?

Change requires courage. David Whyte says, "Courage is what love looks like when tested by the simple everyday necessities of being alive."[10] To be alive is to continue to put myself out there and push myself even when I sense fear. Evolution requires discomfort and risk.

Making Choices

Change happens from the inside out, not the other way around. You begin by changing the dynamics within yourself before ever expecting to see any lasting change outside of yourself. You have to stop pointing the finger at someone else to change first. When we take responsibility and shift ourselves, people around us begin to shift as well—that's especially true for leaders. There are no shortcuts to leadership.

If we as leaders want to change organizational culture, we must start with our own actions and beliefs. If we're trying to be more customer focused, focus on beliefs in dealing with customers. Are customers outside the organization's sphere of control or are they an integral part of how you do business? What are the values you have around customers? What are the values (and actions) you need to change? How can you lead that change?

---

10 David Whyte, *Consolations: The Solace, Nourishment, and Underlying Meaning of Everyday Words* (Langley, WA: Many Rivers Press, 2015), 26.

It takes courage for a leader to say, "I want to change. I want to act differently and lead my team differently." It takes even more courage to say, "What's happening today doesn't work. I know I can do something different, and I'm willing to put myself out there and try as a model for others." There's a reason that seventy percent of change initiatives fail.[11] The work needed to make change happen is difficult and risky, but what's the alternative? Stagnation and extinction.

Having a growth mindset allows people to thrive during some of the most challenging times of their lives. We can apply this just as easily to the challenges facing the modern world of work. Leaders who truly act from a growth-based mindset don't have to prove they're better than others. They don't claim credit for other people's contributions. They don't undermine others to feel successful themselves. They don't need to.

Growth mindset leaders don't have to be the big fish; instead, they are able to surround themselves with the best talent they can find and seek to grow together with that talent. These leaders can look intently and seriously at their deficiencies and try to find ways to improve. They can get feedback and develop the skills needed to take the company into the future. As Carol Dweck so eloquently

---

11   Nitin Nohria and Michael Beer, "Cracking the Code of Change," Harvard Business Review Change Management, May-June 2000, http://hbr.org/2000/05/cracking-the-code-of-change.

says, "Growth-minded leaders...start with a belief in human potential and development—both their own and other people's. Instead of using the company as a vehicle for their greatness, they use it as an engine of growth—for themselves, the employees, and the company as a whole."[12]

THE TRUST MINDSET

Along with connection and growth, another interrelated belief at the heart of evolving leaders is letting go of the need for certainty. In the past, world markets and events have been much more predictable and routine. That's not the case today. The world is changing fast, and none of us know what's around the next bend. Being comfortable with ambiguity and the unknown might sound like a cliché, but it's difficult and powerful to do in practice.

Letting go of the need to know what's coming is one of the deepest challenges I face as an analytical person. At times, I long for the security that comes with having the answer; I also know this belief is the most prominent thing standing in my way. Once I truly let go of the need for certainty and endless details, the best courses of action emerge without me forcing them to happen.

Peter Drucker was one of the first prominent thinkers to

12 Dweck, *Mindset*, 159.

call out our need to face the realities of uncertainty. His statements have immense implications for how we operate within most organizations. Drucker states, "Uncertainty—in the economy, society, politics—has become so great as to render futile, if not counterproductive, the kind of planning most companies still practice: forecasting based on probabilities."[13]

Letting go of this need to control and predict means developing trust in yourself, your team, and the ability to adapt and change even when you don't have all the answers. Trust becomes a great litmus test as an indicator of your evolution as a leader. Do you trust your team to make good decisions, or do you micromanage their tasks and constantly tell them what to do? In terms of your own internal struggle with change, how much do you trust versus how much do you feel you need to control? Do decisions on the team happen organically, in the moment, as the environment signals change? Or are decisions a lagging activity based on what was planned at the beginning of the year?

I'd recommend asking yourself a few additional questions to assist you in your own self-awareness around trust and comfort with ambiguity: Do you withdraw from uncertainty or use it to challenge your own growth? Are you attempting to control the uncontrollable from your own need for power and certainty at work? Do you trust your

---

13   Peter Drucker, "Planning for Uncertainty," *The Wall Street Journal*, July 22, 1992.

own ability to navigate situations that are complex and full of uncertainty?

The ability to navigate uncertainty is one of the reasons many organizations are moving to self-management, leaning into trust in a whole new way. At traditional organizations, strategy begins at the top, with only a few minds in a small room with a plan that then cascades down throughout the rest of the organization. A few executives have the power to control the organization, but the decisions are slow and limited by what the executives personally know. In self-managing organizations, new strategies can come from any person who senses change is needed.

Buurtzorg, the home care provider with the stellar love-based culture, is a great example. Local teams are responsible for decisions they feel best meet customer needs and the organization's mission. For example, nurses within the local community noticed the primary care-givers for their patients needed a break from the daily demands of providing round-the-clock care. In response, they created a bed and breakfast-like boarding house where patients can receive care and caregivers can get a much-needed break. There was no strategic plan to grow the organization in this way. There was no high-level dictate saying they needed a boarding house. Instead, the local level sensed the need, and the team took ownership.

That path ultimately benefited both the patients and the caregivers.[14]

In the face of uncertainty, it's important not to default to control but instead to trust. Leaders must be able to trust their colleagues working on the front line to say what's needed and offer solutions. There, they know best.

Sense and Respond

Being able to let go of control and power gives the organization as a whole the ability to sense what's going on around us and respond in the moment. Everyone is given the opportunity to learn, adapt, experiment, and innovate with events as they happen without the need to control them out of fear.

Scribe was founded in 2014 by Tucker Max and Zach Obront. Max took on the role of CEO as many founders do. A year and a half into the life of the company, they were growing fast and making good money. However, there was a glitch. Max was not succeeding as CEO. Despite the growth, there was significant tension and struggle. Over time, it became clear he was not the guy to take Scribe to the next level. He had to ask himself tough questions.

---

14 "Self-Management," Reinventing Organizations Wiki: A Wiki to Inspire Next Generation Organizations, accessed April 26, 2018, http://www.reinventingorganizationswiki.com/ Self-Management.

"Do I want to have a great company or do I want to be in charge? Is this about me or the mission?"

In the end, Max resigned as CEO and hired someone externally to take the organization forward. Turns out, letting go of control and trusting his instincts and the feedback from the team was the best move possible. In just over a year, the new CEO, JT McCormick, took the company from 50 to 450 books and multiplied the company's revenue many times over.[15]

The story exemplifies the importance of letting go, trusting the path as it unfolds, and tapping into the growth mindset as a way to learn even through deeply difficult situations. Having a leader be vulnerable, facing his own limitations rather than fighting for power, saying, "I'm going to let someone else take the reins," takes a radical new belief. As events showed, however, the decision was absolutely correct.

I recently came across a powerful quote from Pixar CEO Ed Catmull. He said:

> I believe the best managers acknowledge and make room for what they do not know—not just because humility is a virtue, but because until one adopts that mindset, the most striking breakthroughs cannot

---

15   Tucker Max, interview by Heather Hanson, October 13, 2017.

occur. I believe that managers must loosen controls, not tighten them. They must accept risk; they must trust the people they work with and strive to clear the path for them; and always, they must pay attention to and engage with anything that creates fear. Moreover, successful leaders embrace the reality that their models may be wrong or incomplete. Only when we admit what we don't know can we ever hope to learn it.[16]

By making space for the unknown, by letting go of control and top-down hierarchical power, we are able to trust, and in trusting, to respond more easily and fully to a changing world.

THE PURPOSE MINDSET

Our last critical belief system for evolved leaders revolves around *purpose*. Foremost, I talk about purpose as distinct from the typical emphasis on profit. Unfortunately, we're programmed as leaders to believe in pursuit of profit and the power of money as the sole motivating force. In truth, people are only loosely motivated by money. Even conventional wisdom shows that a raise will only continue to make a worker happy for a short while. In contrast, purpose, or a mission larger than ourselves, is a key motivator for all of us over the long term.

---

16   Ed Catmull and Amy Wallace, *Creativity, Inc.* (New York: Random House, 2014), 13.

Purpose creates loyalty and commitment among employees and customers. Moreover, it also creates lasting organizations. In *The Purpose Economy*, Aaron Hurst refers to purpose as the new driving force of the economy, saying it's become a true business imperative, not just a nice-to-have perk. He goes on to say, "The purpose economy is defined by the quest for people to have more purpose in their lives, suggesting it's an economy where value lies in establishing purpose for employees and customers through serving their needs greater than their own, enabling personal growth and building community."[17]

All people desire to be part of something larger than themselves. By providing opportunities for meaning and purpose at work, we as leaders appeal to the deepest motivations of workers and give them opportunities to connect with the organization on a deep level of fulfillment. Leaders who can lead from purpose rather than a sole pursuit of profit will find their people aligned and engaged, and the purpose providing an important competitive advantage.

The book *Firms of Endearment: How World Class Companies Profit from Passion and Purpose* shows that purpose-driven organizations significantly outperform profit-only-focused organizations. The author cites a study over the course of fifteen years of both private and public firms.

---

17 Aaron Hurst, *The Purpose Economy: How Your Desire for Impact, Personal Growth, and Community Is Changing the World* (Boise: Elevate, 2014), 37.

[Purpose-driven public firms] returned 1,026 percent for investors over ten years ending June 30, 2006, compared to 122 percent for the S&P 500. That's more than an eight to one ratio.[18]

Such hard data impacting the bottom line proves organizations don't need to solely exist to maximize shareholder value. Profit can be balanced with other important needs, such as being a positive force for good in the world. An emergent community of changemakers are using purpose in just this way to shape the next generation of organizations. When you're able to define a purpose for the organization that people can get behind, it unites your team. Furthermore, having clear purpose often attracts customers in a virtuous cycle.

Organizations such as Patagonia and Southwest Airlines are forging success out of purpose statements that speak to employees and customers alike. Here are some examples:

- Build the best product, cause no unnecessary harm, use business to inspire and implement solutions to the environmental crisis. (Patagonia)[19]
- To connect People to what's important in their lives

18 Sisodia, Sheth, and Wolfe, *Firms of Endearment*, 54.

19 "Patagonia's Mission Statement," Patagonia, accessed May 2, 2018, http://www.patagonia.com/company-info.html.

through friendly, reliable, and low-cost air travel. (Southwest Airlines)[20]

- We fulfill dreams of personal freedom. (Harley Davidson)[21]
- Provide places for people to flourish. (Decurion)[22]
- We are a global design company committed to creating positive impact. (IDEO)[23]

The statements speak not only to what they do but why they do it and how they impact the world around them. As the evidence from *Firms of Endearment* shows so clearly, we now know that in the long term, the most successful organizations move past profit maximization to serve a purpose greater than their own self-interest. These organizations are using the powerful force of capitalism to support communities, societies, and the planet, as well as those who work for the organization. This allows people to connect with the organization in a much different way because it's more than just doing a job; it's a mission and a reason for being.

Moving to a Purpose Mindset

Purpose, and the pursuit of work that's meaningful to us, is the glue that binds so many of these beliefs together. The other mindsets—the incredible trust needed to identify and follow your purpose, to choose a different path, and to face fear—are highly interrelated with purpose. Rather than going to work only to get a paycheck, in embracing a purpose mindset you make the shift to find your true north, to live a life of integrity, and to bring your beliefs and values into alignment with your actions. The purpose of work and your purpose become aligned in powerful ways.

In my consulting and coaching work, I've found one of the most challenging situations for clients is standing up for what they believe in, speaking their truths. We are so often fearful of being judged in the workplace or being labeled as an outcast. Truly evolved leaders learn how to take this fear and use it instead for self-awareness, growth, and compassion, channeling this dynamic into creating love-based environments that allow people to fully show up. They create places of fulfillment, where individuals can realize their purpose and, in exchange, reap tremendous gains in business terms.

Unravel the Stranglehold of Fear

We are at a point in time when we all need to learn how to stand on our own two feet again. We need to see fear for what it is and accurately identify how it limits our potential and experience at work. When we begin to embrace and embody these four powerful beliefs, we begin to unravel the stranglehold of fear.

With the mindset of human connection, growth, trust and purpose, we begin to have the courage to articulate how our individual role connects to the larger purpose of the organization and how the work helps move the mission forward.

We must have the courage to speak up even when it could be contrary to norms or beliefs widely held within the culture.

To lead in this evolved space, we have to take back our responsibility, lean in to authentic self-expression, and find our shared purpose in the work that's meaningful to all of us. In the world of fear and control that most organizations operate in, to lead from love is a courageous—and necessary—act.

CHAPTER FIVE

Leadership Practices

DELIBERATE STEPS FORWARD

As you begin to examine your leadership beliefs and mindsets, there are exercises and practices that will help you along the way. I'd encourage you first, though, not to go it alone. Due to our natural biases and mental models, we all need help getting beyond ourselves and the beliefs and assumptions we hold. Outside perspectives help show us our beliefs and point out our limitations. Having a person who challenges you and shows you your blind spots is a huge advantage in developing new leadership beliefs and behaviors. I am a professional coach who has a coach for this very reason. To best serve my clients, I must continually examine my own beliefs and expand my awareness.

Developing new leadership beliefs and practices requires a

holistic process, not a one-day Myers-Briggs workshop or a one-and-done session with a coach. We must develop a genuine desire and practice around deep self-awareness. Leadership growth is about lifelong learning and action.

In this chapter, I will highlight four specific practices that will help you as you move along a path to broaden your level of awareness and deepen your leadership. In more than ten years of work with leaders and organizations, I have found these practices, of all I have tried, to be the most impactful, though of course there are many other effective practices I would encourage you to seek out and try.

Let's begin with the foundation needed to use the practices effectively: awareness. Awareness can be both internal and external, seeing ourselves clearly and knowing how others view us, but in this book, I chose to focus on the internal awareness that makes the most difference to leadership growth.

CULTIVATING AWARENESS

Author Pema Chodron says, "The most fundamental harm we can do to ourselves is to remain ignorant by not having the courage and the respect to look at ourselves honestly and gently."[1] That is what self-awareness is about: taking

---

1 Pema Chodron, *When Things Fall Apart: Heart Advice for Difficult Times* (Boulder, CO: Shambala Publications, Inc., 2000), 31.

a good look at yourself in a loving, kind way that allows you to grow.

Internal awareness is often misunderstood. We imagine that everyone else knows and perceives us the way we do. We don't recognize why our good intentions are so poorly received. Our blind spots limit us. Dr. Tasha Eurich finds, "The more power we attain, the less self-aware we tend to be."[2] Executives face a very dangerous situation: the higher you rise on the corporate ladder, the less likely others are to tell you the truth. Self-awareness becomes a critical ingredient for success.

Let's play out an example. A leader may show up in a meeting with the good intention of keeping the team up to date on new developments. In so doing, he or she speaks *at* the meeting participants for an entire hour, leaving little room for any other perspectives or contributions. This leader is likely missing social cues from around the room—arms folded across the chest, others responding to email, blank stares. When leaders are not able to recognize their impact on others, they are going to quickly lose their effectiveness and their ability to learn. Often, what results from an example like this is those attending feel devalued, that they have no room to speak

---

2   Victor Lipman, "Do higher-level leaders have lower self-awareness?" Forbes. com, April 17, 2018, https://www.forbes.com/sites/victorlipman/2018/04/17/do-higher-level-leaders-have-lower-self-awareness/#6407b5e15a8b.

or contribute, which ultimately creates an environment of disengagement.

As a leader, to be effective, you must be consistent, and that means you must have a heightened level of awareness. Many leaders I've worked with struggle with consistency in decisions, behaviors, and day-to-day actions due to a lack of clarity around their values and a lack of guardrails to guide decisions. Without these key anchors, leadership can appear random. One day, the team is instructed to move in this direction only to find out that direction changes the following week. One set of emotional reactions prevails today, but another shows up tomorrow. When individuals are unable to predict you, they're likely to be afraid of you or disconnected from you as a result.

However, if you consistently operate from a place of clearly articulated values, people understand you and have the safety of knowing who's going to show up each day. Values and awareness impact your ability to effectively lead.

Self-awareness pays off personally as well. Eurich finds that "people who are high in internal self-awareness tend to make choices consistent with who they really are, allowing them to lead happier, more satisfying lives."[3] Gaining self-awareness allows us to win in both work and life.

---

3   Tasha Eurich, *Insight: How Small Gains in Self-Awareness Can Help You Win Big in Work and in Life* (New York: Crown Business,2017), 15.

THE PRACTICES

How do you cultivate self-awareness? How do you turn that self-awareness into guiding values, passions, and aspirations that inform your leadership? Put simply, you practice.

I've included four leadership practices in this chapter: a values audit, a purpose discovery, an exercise discovering your growth edge, and the practice of mindfulness. These are the practices I've found to be most impactful for moving people through change, expanding consciousness, and providing clarity to move forward in a more purposeful way. All are abbreviated to get you started. Working with a good coach will help you get the depth and fullness out of each of these exercises.

I will offer one caveat before we explore the practices in depth. As you progress on a journey of deep leader development, you will experience bumps in the road. It can be challenging to shift your leadership while remaining in the same role and the same organization. The analogy of rising floors in the apartment building from Chapter 3 is especially poignant here. As you rise in your levels of awareness and consciousness, the world around you changes. You must face new and challenging questions about your work as well as pressure and doubt from those around you. It is completely possible to shift and change your leadership within your current role, but don't be surprised if you begin to feel uneasy within your current position.

When you begin to experiment with new practices, pay attention to the reaction of those around you. Do you experience support or resistance? Is your boss open to you exploring new ways of leading? Are your colleagues open, receptive, and curious about what you are doing? Or are you experiencing ridicule and dismissal as you expand your thinking? These are all signs to help you determine if your current environment is a good place for you to continue your growth. The reality, however, is that some in stifling situations end up leaving their roles because the environment no longer supports their growth and development. The best path forward may require a change to find a supportive environment where you can do the work you need to do to evolve. Pay attention to how your environment reacts to your change. This will be a great teacher for you as you move forward.

Let's begin with the first practice.

THE VALUES AUDIT

Understanding our values plays a pivotal role in our success as leaders. But first, let's differentiate between beliefs and values. Beliefs are assumptions we hold to be true, and they arise from our experiences. Values, on the other hand, are based on what we deem important and are driven specifically from our needs. Values can often stem from our beliefs, as our experiences drive what we deem to be important. Values drive thoughts, words, and actions. In essence, values are the language of why. They are important parts of who you are and why you do what you do at work.

Ignoring your values at work oftentimes leads to frustrating experiences and dissatisfaction, especially if the values you hold conflict with the values demonstrated at work. Notice that I'm not talking about the value statements in brochures and painted on the walls. I'm talking about what's demonstrated in action.

Values are powerful when they are actionable and aligned. Decision-making becomes easy when values guide the way. This is not a new concept. Organizations have been doing values audits for years. There are several tools for doing personal inventories of what's important to you from a values perspective. However, when values are empty words or statements that don't translate into everyday action, they aren't helpful. I'd encourage you to slow down and think deeply here and to come back to the audit periodically. It's common for values to change as our lives and priorities change.

Why Are Values Important?

Once you know what your values are, you're able to more accurately assess if they're in alignment with your role and the organization's values. When you work in an organization that naturally aligns with your values, you feel a sense of connection, belonging, and freedom. This in turn creates a great deal of intrinsic motivation to go above and beyond in service of the shared goals, which is what great leaders and businesses strive for.

In *Corporate Culture and Performance*, authors John Kotter and James Heskett show that over a decade, purpose- and value-driven companies outperform their counterparts in stock price by a factor of twelve.[4] Living from a place of values and purpose demonstrably leads to much greater bottom-line effects for organizations.

Peter Senge also talks about this in his book *The Fifth Discipline*.[5] He suggests to create a learning organization that survives and prospers over time, people need to feel that their own vision and values are inherently connected to the company's vision and values.

---

4   Hayley Leibson, "The Power of Purpose-Driven," Forbes.com Entrepreneurs #ChangetheWorld, January 25, 2018, https://www.forbes.com/sites/hayleyleibson/2018/01/25/the-power-of-purpose-driven/2/#2973f35e3b6c.

5   Peter M. Senge, *The Fifth Discipline: The Art & Practice of the Learning Organization* (New York: Doubleday, 2006).

Values Audit Exercise

I'd strongly encourage you to take action toward understanding the values driving your own behavior and your team's behaviors in the organization. The Barrett Values Center has a free personal values assessment (PVA) you can take that links your results back to the levels of leadership consciousness previously discussed in this book. You can take the assessment for free at this link: http://www.valuescentre.com/our-products/products-individuals/personal-values-assessment-pva.

Step One

Find a discovery tool to help you identify the values most important to you in the context of your leadership and career. The PVA mentioned above is a great place to start, or you can find a variety of values cards that you can sort and prioritize to get a clearer sense of your top values. Once you identify what's most important to you, expand out from the specific words with context. Identifying a word or phrase is great, but you get much greater meaning when you define the value further or give a concrete example. If one of your core values is health, you might describe health as "living with vitality and energy every day" or, in terms of actions, eating a healthy diet and exercising regularly. Making your definition concrete is an important step, as it provides detail for you to evaluate how and if you are living in alignment with your values.

Step Two

Begin to test your values to see if they make sense for your leadership and career. There are times when values may begin to shift due to deeper learning. Ask yourself, does this value truly feel consistent with how you want to lead and the leader you want to be? Does it feel true to how you want to live? Does it still hold value for you? These little gut checks can help you gauge if the value still drives decisions in your life and for your leadership.

If we don't examine and articulate our core values, they remain unconscious drivers of our behavior. Only when we take the time to clearly state what we hold dear can we begin to bring consistency and purpose to our daily behaviors. By using refining questions—"Is this really important to me?" "Is this true to how I make decisions?" "In a tough situation, will I choose to act in this way?"—the values become more clear and actionable in our day-to-day lives.

Step Three

Begin to use each of your core values intentionally in your decision-making. Oftentimes, we take our values for granted and don't use them to guide our decisions. We use whatever data is in front of us and forget to tap into the more innate truth. In my own life, being able to make decisions based on my core values always leads to a better result because my values are a deeper reflection of who I am and what I believe.

Think about big or small decisions you need to make, and consider these in light of your top five values. How can your values guide your decision-making? What direction would they lead you in? Personal values are an important element to your career. When they align with the organization's values, there's great synergy between what you're good at, what you love, and what the world needs. The alignment creates focus and energy, which is why this exploration is so important.

Problems arise when there is significant conflict between the values of an individual and the values of an organization. More often than not, those conflicts go unresolved in traditional organizations, explaining the disengagement and suffering at work we've discussed. At progressive organizations, value conversations are becoming more and more welcome and considered an integral part of one's growth and development with an organization.

For example, an organization might have a value that says the customer is always right. An individual employee may have some valid reasons for why that value isn't always true. Evolved Executives allow that tension to become a conversation between leaders and employees so everyone can understand why it exists, why it's creating conflict, and how they can collectively move through it. Often, the team can find a solution or resolution that feels whole for everyone, which is a healthy outcome. Sometimes, if there is an inherent value conflict that can't be resolved, an individual might need to find a better fit, whether that means leaving the organization or finding a different role—that's also a successful outcome. Identifying the conflict and engaging in conversation to identify a solution to the conflict is hands down better than just suffering in the toxicity.

People who don't have a clear idea of their values tend to be on autopilot in their career. They lack language to talk about what's most important to them, and the framework with which to make decisions in line with their deepest desires. As a result, often, their careers happen to them rather than them intentionally choosing to build and shape a career that's right and good for their soul.

Values turn out to be extremely important. They give us context with which to make strong decisions, language to have meaningful conversations, and a compass by which to build a career. Moreover, in the uncertain and ambiguous environment we all live in, values provide a guiding light and a critical tool with which to lead. As such, I'd strongly encourage you to dive deeply in the value audit to uncover your core truths, which will innately and effectively inform your sense of purpose.

THE PURPOSE DISCOVERY

This practice of discovering one's purpose has been around for some time. Even so, when put to good use, finding your purpose is an exceptionally powerful leadership exercise. Simon Sinek, one of the greatest experts and advocates in this area, published his seminal book *Start with Why* in 2009.[6] This work has made tremendous impact in corporations around the world, and yet, when I work one-on-one with leaders, I find most people only skim the surface of his message and guidance. To find one's why requires a deep inquiry into your life's story, time to reflect on it, and the courage to succinctly put to words what matters most for you. It's important to go deep into the process to discover your true why, both for your own good and for those you lead.

People tend to get stuck looking for their purpose. They think their purpose is going to be something that dawns on them in the middle of the night, allowing them to live out the rest of their lives with crystal clear clarity. Discovering your purpose in life is actually an active process, and it can change over time. You need to experiment to understand what brings you joy and energy and what drains the life out of you. Purpose is not something you can figure out in your head through thinking deep thoughts alone. Trust me, I've tried to do it that way, and it doesn't work. You

---

6   Simon Sinek, *Start with Why: How Great Leaders Inspire Everyone to Take Action* (New York: Penguin Group, 2009).

find your purpose by living life and by examining the life you have lived.

The writer Mark Manson has some intriguing questions for helping people find their life purpose, one of which is, "What makes you forget to eat and poop?"[7] What will grab your attention and not let it go? You've likely had experiences when you forgot to eat because you were so engaged in something that time flew by. Those experiences fuel and inspire you. On the other hand, when something is causing you to suffer, it's important to stop doing that thing. Make a different choice. That's part of the process of finding your purpose: if what you're doing today is clearly not it, try something else.

The Purpose Discovery Exercise

I have found a process that marries the head and the heart to guide leaders in uncovering their purpose. The following comes from my work experience and my personal journey of finding my own purpose, as well as inspiration from Simon Sinek's *Start with Why* and George and Sim's *Finding Your True North.*[8] Discovering your why is

---

7   Mark Manson. "7 Strange Questions That Help You Find Your Life Purpose," September 18, 2014, https://markmanson.net/life-purpose.

8   Bill George and Peter Sims, *True North: Discover your Authentic Leadership* (San Francisco: Jossey Bass, 2007).

a beautiful journey of uncovering your authentic self and in doing so, uncovering your authentic leadership.

There are four steps to get you started moving through the why discovery process.

Step One

Begin by understanding deeply who you are and what's important to you. Tell your story.

In George's book, Howard Schultz, the CEO of Starbucks, says, "The reservoir of all my life experiences shaped me as a person and a leader."[9] Your life experiences, too, are where the magic is. Spend some time remembering and recording the pivotal moments that have left lasting and meaningful impressions: moments of pain, embarrassment, and sorrow, as well as joy, exhilaration, and freedom. All are your story.

As you tell your story, it's important to look not only at the bright spots but also at the times when you were challenged or when you struggled. Think both about the stories that you tell others and the stories you really don't want others to know. Look for events that make you feel excited, proud, frustrated, or angry—the ones with emotion. Some of the most painful times are the most important in terms

9   George and Sims, *True North*, 5.

of guiding your life. George refers to these as "crucibles."[10] They are times of illness, death, discrimination, fear, frustration, and sorrow. By reflecting on these events, you can understand yourself, your values, and your purpose in a different light.

Be prepared for some pain with the inquiry and the exploration that goes along with understanding who you are at a deep level. It might hurt to go back into stories where you've experienced pain, sorrow, frustration, or disappointment. Lean into the discomfort to really understand the lesson and use it to guide your life forward. It's not all pain—there is a lot of joy in finding what creates passion and inspiration for you as an individual and as a leader. Only by going through these exercises, the joyful and the difficult, can you get clarity around who you are and discover the gifts you can share with the world.

Common themes and patterns emerge often in these stories. Pay attention. You might get six or seven stories down and start to think, "Oh my goodness, I never realized mentoring others was such a huge part of my life." The themes that continue to show up in your stories are the values that are guiding your life.

Some questions to think about as you reflect on your stories: What lessons did I learn? What made me happy?

---

10   George and Sims, *True North*, xiv.

What made me disappointed? Why was it important? What was lacking? Who was with me? Ask whatever questions will help you get to the core of the story so you can see the patterns. Journaling helps as you dive deeper into some of the stories.

Share these stories with someone you trust. Oftentimes, an objective person can hear and see themes you might not. A coach can be helpful. In my practice with clients, I am the person who gets the opportunity to reflect back the themes. They get to be in the story, and I offer perspective on what is emerging in the larger picture.

Step Two

This step is about paying attention to the feedback you get from those around you, a huge part of the process of becoming self-aware. Think of feedback from others as additional data points to add to the story of your life. Ask, what feedback do I consistently receive—the good, bad, and ugly—from colleagues, my boss, my peers? What does that feedback tell me about who I am and what's important to me?

Similarly, ask others what they would say is your purpose. What are you uniquely skilled and positioned to do in the world? Objective perspectives can be more powerful than your own, even though feedback can be difficult to hear. In my own life, for years, people told me my true talent was as a coach and expert consultant. I resisted that with all my might. I'd been in the corporate setting for decades and saw a lot of poor coaches and ineffective consultants come in and try to give a silver-bullet answer. I knew in my core that was not an effective strategy, and I struggled with the idea of being a coach and consultant until I realized that I didn't have to be limited by my own stereotypes. I could help people in the ways I knew to be right, letting my own gifts shine to truly help my clients.

I encourage you to reflect more deeply on anything people tell you that you are resisting. Those very things could be incredible teachers for you as you think about defining your purpose.

Step Three

The third step is revisiting and finalizing your themes. Based on everything you've uncovered from your life stories, crucible moments, and feedback from others, find the elements most critical to your success and fulfillment. Ask, what are the contributions I want to make in the world? What legacy do I want to leave, and what's the impact? Of everything I have learned, what is the most important?

It can be difficult to choose the most important elements,

but this is the critical piece for growth. If you're journaling, go back and circle these as they stand out to you. You may have fifteen themes, but for this part of the process, you're going to have to cull them down to five—or fewer.

Step Four

The last step, which everyone is excited to get to, is creating a guiding statement that says, "This is who I am today, and why I do what I do."

Here is an example. After months of working on my own purpose discovery process, I finally found the statement that is true for me. My purpose is "to awaken the souls of leaders so we can create soulful organizations."

Being able to create a simple and concise statement is exceptionally powerful; it focuses you and allows you to get excited about what you're doing in the world. A purpose statement guides your decisions, and clarifies your priorities. The key is to make it simple and clear. If it doesn't powerfully resonate with you, go back and try again.

There is one caveat: I believe the most powerful purpose statements are those that are in service of others. We have so much baggage from the Industrial Revolution mindset, during which our value was primarily measured through our individual contributions, and so it becomes difficult to look beyond ourselves. However, as an Evolved Executive, it is important to recognize that leadership is about serving others. In *Give and Take*, author, researcher, and Wharton professor Adam Grant uncovered that leaders who focus on helping others create stronger teams, better relationships, and a better bottom line for their companies. Love in action is, more often than not, about being in service to others.[11]

THE GROWTH EDGE

This is where things get more challenging. The first two exercises are foundational and well known in the field, but they don't get used to the depth of their true potential. The growth edge, on the other hand, is an exercise that is not as well known. The growth edge is about becoming familiar with the parts inside of us, the habits, assumptions, and behaviors that keep us stuck. This learning often makes us feel like we're at the edge of a cliff; we can choose to stay in our comfort zone where it feels safe, or we can take a leap into the unknown. When we're moving beyond our old ways of being, we must let go of our fears and lean into growth, which ultimately opens up new potential, skills, and opportunities in our lives. I was first introduced to this work by Robert Kegan and Lisa Laskow Lahey in their

---

11   Adam Grant, *Give and Take: Why Helping Others Drives Our Success* (New York: Penguin Books, 2014).

book *The Immunity to Change*[12] and then subsequently completed a thorough deep dive myself with an incredible learning community called LeadWise Academy.

Becoming an Evolved Executive requires that we take a good look at our belief systems and assumptions and be willing to let them go in pursuit of evolving and growing to be a more conscious leader. This exercise becomes an important part of that process, but it is challenging. As we move through the process, it's very common to cringe as we begin to uncover the limiting beliefs and recognize how these beliefs manifest in actions which block us from change. This was absolutely my experience as well.

The process requires that you uncover your "one big thing," that stubborn and nagging obstacle in your path of improving your leadership. This is not a surface-level behavior that you just noticed, but rather an ongoing challenge and deep belief that you need to work on. It is often something you've worked on in the past that continues to trip you up.

The Growth Edge Exercise

Growth requires that we be willing to push outside of our zone of comfort, to work on the very edge of what

---

12 Robert Kegan and Lisa Laskow Lahey, *Immunity to Change: How to Overcome It and Unlock the Potential in Yourself and your Organization* (Brighton, MA: Harvard Business School Publishing Corporation, 2009).

we think we are capable of achieving and changing in our lives. This exercise is designed to help you begin this process, and will do so by offering you a simple framework to tackle a goal that matters to you. When you begin to embrace change, you will be confronted with the very beliefs and behaviors that get in your way. You have the opportunity to examine your internal motivations—the desire to avoid failure, to be perfect, to escape conflict or to simply remain in the safety of what you know. When you become open to letting go of these attachments, you will find change will become easier.

During the growth edge exercise, you go through four different steps, each giving you new insight and the chance to dive into different parts of who you are. You can access a template provided by Harvard University to guide you along in this process here: https://www.extension.harvard.edu/inside-extension/surprising-reason-we-dont-keep-our-resolutions-how-overcome-it.[13]

Step One

Identify a goal that feels important to you, something you want to change or get better at. Avoid choosing a technical skill (i.e. improving my knowledge of PowerPoint). To get

---

13   For the template, see "The Surprising Reason We Don't Keep Our
     Resolutions (and How to Overcome It)," Harvard Extension School, accessed
     May 1, 2018, https://www.extension.harvard.edu/inside-extension/
     surprising-reason-we-dont-keep-our-resolutions-how-overcome-it.

the greatest benefit from this practice, dig deeper to find a truly meaningful goal. Here is a good example: "I'm committed to getting better at courageous authenticity. I need to take tough stands, bring up hard conversations, tell the truth with love, and ask for what I need."

Take the time to really think through this step. Choosing the right goal, the goal that feels meaningful and daunting at once, is important. Choose something that is blocking you from being your best self at work, something unique to who you are.

Step Two

Identify behavior blockers. Ask yourself, what am I doing to actively work against this goal? What am I not doing that would actually help me achieve this goal? Take an honest self-inventory of your counterproductive behaviors. What do you do that ensures you aren't getting the desired goal in your life? What are you doing in support of the goal? What do you need to start doing to help you change?

To continue with the example of courageous authenticity (telling your truth and standing up for yourself), in Step 2, your behavior blockers might be not speaking up, holding back when you should be direct, letting others make decisions for you, and avoiding confrontation. All of these behaviors are simple, day-to-day actions getting in the way of the goal you want to achieve. Behavior blockers are often habits that we fall into over time without consideration.

Be honest with yourself about what you do, then brainstorm ways to change those behaviors, starting with small, easy steps.

Step Three

Step Three is about competing commitments. This work is difficult, so take it deliberately and with dedication. In the template, you'll see a box, which I lovingly refer to as "the dreaded worry box." Once you've faced all your sabotaging behavior patterns from Step 2, it becomes important to understand their purpose. In this step, you imagine doing the opposite of the behavior you just listed. What are the biggest worries or fears that arise when you imagine yourself doing the opposite of your habit?

Back to the example, the opposite of holding back when you should be direct is, not surprisingly, speaking up or being direct. Imagine doing that, and see what thoughts and emotions arise. You might worry you'll be disliked, alone, or rejected. You might worry that you'll appear incompetent or that you'll lose the regard of those close to you or that you'll have to face conflict. Those fears feel too terrible to face, and so you fail to speak directly.

The worry box is an important step. Don't skip it! Rarely does anyone achieve transformational change simply by reflecting. The change you want to see is completely within your own control, but it takes work and honesty. It's not someone else holding you back; you're holding yourself back. You must understand the root fears and beliefs to untangle the current situation and achieve a new outcome.

Next, dive into your hidden commitments, those unconscious commitments you make to yourself so you don't have to feel a certain way or look a certain way to others. For example, your hidden commitment might be that you avoid decisions that make you disliked, put aside opinions so you're seen as competent, or avoid the whole conversation so you don't create conflict. What do you do so you don't feel things you don't want to feel?

Again, this activity begins to highlight the behaviors and beliefs holding you back from the change you want to see in your life and leadership.

Step Four

The last step is to jot down your big assumptions, which help reveal the core beliefs that keep you stuck. As you reflect on each of your hidden commitments, complete the sentence, "I may be assuming that..." to get yourself started. For example, I may have a hidden commitment to avoid situations or conversations that could result in conflict. In that case, "I may be assuming that... conflict is bad and needs to be avoided ...or I can control how others feel about me or react to me." Kegan and Lahey say that we have an immune system within us that resists change.[14] When we look at our assumptions in this way, we allow insight into the system of beliefs that hold us in place and keep us from changing.

Take a good look at these assumptions, put them on the table, consider and explore them, and decide if you want them to stay in your life. You might assume others are always more competent than you, that conflict is bad, or that being wrong or failing must be avoided. Test your assumptions to see if they are true. See what happens when you intentionally choose a different behavior. For example, if you assume conflict is bad, find a situation that you would normally avoid and make the exceptional effort to engage versus escape. Have that difficult conversation with a colleague that you've been avoiding. Bring up a challenging topic at work that has been bothering you. Find a situation that often gets you stuck and see if you can change how you approach it. Treat this process as an experiment for you to learn. Start small—in a situation where the stakes are small—and work up to harder interactions.

---

14   Kegan and Lahey, *Immunity to Change*, 36.

Collect data. After you have the conversation, ask the individual how it went. Do a self-check as well. Ask yourself, how did it feel to address this conflict directly? Was it as bad as you thought? Did it cause pain? Did it hurt your career? Was it liberating? Did it create some other emotions? Test your assumptions to see if they were true or false.

Often, seeing that many of our deepest worries about our actions are, in fact, false can be a tremendously liberating process. To get there, however, you must be willing to walk into the fear and to test it.

MINDFULNESS

I recommend mindfulness to all my clients as a highly effective and necessary practice for evolved leaders, though I do emphasize that it doesn't have to be as formal as much of the press suggests. Mindfulness is simply creating time and space to be, to remove the need to constantly do and rather let go to the silence within.

Our minds have a basic need to take a pause and go silent. No inner knowledge or knowing will surface without this break, because the constant mental chatter will otherwise take over everything. Joe Dispenza, author of *Becoming Supernatural*, says, "If you don't get beyond who you think you are and the way you've become conditioned to believe the world works, it's not possible to create a new life or destiny."[15] The way to get beyond who you think you are is to be mindful. Growth is only possible by taking a pause, recognizing the internal chatter for what it is, and being with the silence where inner knowledge can emerge.

I'm not suggesting everyone take up a rigorous meditation practice. I am suggesting everyone needs a way to quiet their minds to create greater presence and awareness. If meditation is not for you, go for a hike and be present with the birds, the ground, the sky, whatever you see. Bathe in nature. Go for a walk and notice your feet hitting the ground, the sounds of the cars, and the pull of your dog's leash. Take a few moments sitting at your desk to scan through your body bit by bit, getting in touch with the present moment and creating space. Breathe quietly. However we do it, taking ten minutes in the morning or twenty in the evening to calm ourselves and create some silence can be instrumental in our lives.

There is one simple practice I encourage you to try. You have to do it anyway, so why not use it as a way to up your leadership game? Breathe. Taking three deep breaths can do amazing things for your mind, body, and soul, especially when you are experiencing negative emotions such as fear, worry, anxiety, or frustration. A mentor of mine says that we need to recognize the fear between

---

15   Dr. Joe Dispenza, *Becoming Supernatural: How Common People Are Doing the Uncommon* (Carlsbad, CA: Hay House, 2017), 66.

our ears and feel the love in our hearts. By simply taking a deep breath in, feeling the breath expand through our chest, and slowly releasing the breath, we naturally let go of fear, which allows love to expand. You can do this simple practice before a meeting, a difficult conversation, on your way into work, or simply while taking a coffee break. Give it a try!

NO PAIN NO GAIN

Spend the time to go through these practices in depth, even if they are uncomfortable. For the leader who wants to move to the next level, to operate with love in action, continuously improve, be of greater service to others, and lead organizations more fully and holistically, deliberate practice and growth are the only ways. So many things in life are challenging, and growth simply hurts a little. However, it hurts more to stay stagnant.

I believe in you and your journey. Put in the work, and you'll see the outcomes you are looking for.

A TRUSTED COACH

I want to mention again as we finish our discussion of practices that you don't have to go through this process alone. In fact, you may experience greater results with guidance from a trusted coach.

Having someone to work with you as you move through the leadership practices is a huge asset. It's often hard to see yourself objectively as others see you, and it helps having someone with you to guide you in the process, ask good questions, and observe you in action. We know the higher up you are in an organization, the less true feedback you get. A trusted coach is an advocate and ally for your success and will help you see reality from many different perspectives. Unfortunately, we often don't ask for or give ourselves the help we need. Recognize this is also a hidden commitment that limits our success.

Often, leaders carry the belief that a coach is only needed if one is underperforming. In truth, a coach can often be most valuable when you need to accelerate your development, not simply get to average performance. Coaches are trained to support you in finding clarity, purpose and focus, accountability, open and honest feedback, and increased confidence. If you truly desire to move into higher levels of awareness and this next stage of leadership required for today's organizations, consider investing in yourself.

Most of all, don't go it alone.

PART III

Charting the New Organization

CHAPTER SIX

Healing the Organization

DIVE INTO CULTURE

Culture eats strategy for breakfast.

—PETER DRUCKER[1]

You've likely seen or heard this Peter Drucker quote many times before. While it is not often refuted, very few organizations intentionally design their culture. Instead, they move forward hoping enough strategic planning, forecasting, and reporting will drive results.

---

1   This quote is widely cited in a variety of sources. An example: Torben Rick, "Organizational Culture Eats Strategy for Breakfast Lunch and Dinner," Supply Chain 247, Supply Chain News, December 16, 2014, https://www.supplychain247. com/article/organizational_culture_eats_strategy_for_breakfast_lunch_and_dinner/ legacy_supply_chain_services.

Why is this the case? In my experience, culture is often considered the amorphous, squishy thing that is hard to see and "nice to have" but not critical. Culture, in the minds of many executives, has nothing to do with the work that needs to get done.

Unfortunately, that couldn't be further from the truth. Culture is part of the fabric of everyday work, as it's how we "do things" within organizations. Since this is a short chapter on a very intense topic, I would encourage you to find more resources as you need them. I focus here on the critical points for your growth as an Evolved Executive. I offer building blocks to ensure you are equipped to foster the culture you want and not be a victim of the culture you neglect.

ORGANIZATIONAL HEALTH

Look around your organization. When was the last time you paid attention to the health and dynamics of the living, breathing system you call your company? Your employees do the work, but what do you really know about them? When was the last time you checked in on their lives? Do you know what obstacles are in their way? Do you know what gives them a sense of meaning and purpose? Have you asked them for feedback on how you could better support their work?

These aren't the kinds of things managers typically think

about when working to strengthen a culture. However, when employee frustration and disengagement arises, it is likely not because the Playstation in the breakroom is on the fritz or there weren't free sandwiches for lunch. Instead, it is likely due to the problems the questions above illustrate—a lack of clarity around goals, poorly defined roles and decision-making authority, and the lack of communication on important issues. Culture arises from how people, and especially management, treats everyone else.

Too often when we think of exceptional cultures, we think of the Silicon Valley perks—onsite dry cleaning, free breakfast, all-you-can-eat M&M's and popsicles. However, when employees are engaged, it is not often a result of these surface perks; it's a result of open lines of communication, clear and direct linkages between the organization's mission and individual purpose, and a genuine level of trust amongst the leaders and colleagues all around. Culture is about these internal dynamics, which pave the way for effective work to be done.

CONSEQUENCE OF CULTURE

The culture within an organization heavily influences what it can do and how fast. However, culture is not an independent or isolated factor at work. There is a highly dynamic interplay between culture, engagement, and leadership. First, we know that culture breeds engagement or disengagement—the way employees feel about their work and experiences at work. We also know highly engaged units perform better. Engaged employees are more present and productive, they are more attuned to the needs of customers, and they are more observant of processes, standards, and systems. When taken together, the outcomes of highly engaged business units result in 21 percent greater profitability.[2] Engagement can only happen when the culture is open, collaborative, and transparent.

The authors of *Firms of Endearment* say, "A company's culture is a window on the executive's soul."[3] It's true that oftentimes leadership and culture are two sides of the same coin. When an organization begins, the leader has a natural preference for how work gets done. These beliefs and preferences are impressed upon the group and eventually become the operating norms or the culture of the team. So, in a very real sense, leaders create culture.

On the flip side, in a more mature organization, culture will also inform and influence leadership. Here is an example. A new executive is brought in from the outside of an organization to lead a team, but he or she is met with significant resistance and disapproval. This leader may be perceived as too aggressive or outspoken for a specific type of culture or even too meek and timid to influence

---

2   Harter and Mann, "The Right Culture."

3   Sisodia, Sheth, and Wolfe, *Firms of Endearment*, 68.

those in authority. Culture informs the behaviors that are expected for leaders and will greatly impact their success.

OUR ORGANIZATIONS NEED HEALING

Culture, if understood from the perspective of "how we do things around here," becomes an incredible medicine to heal the crisis of suffering in organizations. We've talked about the perils of organizational fear, and in no way is this more important than in the area of culture; a fear-based culture cripples an organization over time. Individuals withhold their perspectives, knowledge, and insights for fear of ridicule; information is hoarded as a power play and command-and-control policies squash motivation and innovation. Fortunately, progressive leaders are beginning to wake up to how critical workplace culture is to the overall health and success of an organization.

Organizations that successfully attract, retain, and engage great workforces are those that focus on culture and well-being in a holistic way. They pay attention to the full spectrum of how culture touches peoples' lives, their health, well-being, autonomy, and purpose, what we've called the system of love in action. Culture is not the narrow, myopic idea that we've believed in the past; it involves every interaction within an organization.

Jeffrey Pfeffer, in his book *Dying for a Paycheck*, finds "what matters for employee engagement and productivity and, more important, for employee physical and mental health, is the work environment and the work itself."[4] He goes on to say, "Not having a boss who heaps scorn and abuse," is critical to the overall health of employees and the organization. However, in his research, several specific areas emerge as central themes to improving the toxicity we experience in many traditional organizations: job control, autonomy, and social support.

Evolved organizations are deeply concerned with these elements: specifically, how people are treated, how people are connected to meaning and purpose, and how power and control can be given to individuals as much as possible. These shifts create a culture that fosters individual freedom and autonomy to do the work at hand and the authority to make the decisions that drive their work. In turn, these organizations have much greater customer satisfaction ratings, more innovation, and as a result more profit, as evidenced by the aforementioned statistics. Building an intentional, love-based culture is one of the best investments you can make.

SERVANT LEADERSHIP AND HEALING

Servant leadership has been discussed in depth in previous chapters, but there is a unique element about this

---

4   Pfeffer, *Dying for a Paycheck*, 153.

approach that makes it especially fitting for healing culture. One of the great strengths of servant leadership is the potential for healing yourself and your relationship to others, leading to a powerful force of transformation in both people and organizations. In most traditional organizations, pervasive suffering has left people with broken spirits and a variety of emotional hurts. Servant leadership recognizes we all have an opportunity to heal through the way we interact with others and our work. We must show up as leaders consciously, being able to do so in a way that appreciates differences and allows people's wholeness and voices to come to light. The next chapter gives specific practices to address this.

Several studies have highlighted how servant leadership can, in fact, improve the overall well-being and emotional health of team members by creating a positive and healthy organizational culture. In "Healing a Broken Spirit: Role of Servant Leadership" the authors find:

> A servant leader—with reported behaviour characteristics such as empathy, compassion, and altruistic calling and healing—builds not only a mentally and emotionally healthy workforce but also inculcates a sense of cohesiveness, collaboration, and sustainable relationships among the followers by understanding and addressing their feelings and emotions... [A servant leader] increases pro-social and altruistic

behaviour among followers that improves organizational performance.[5]

Servant leaders' approach of compassion and care works within organizations to foster healing, well-being, and engagement. This, in turn, leads ultimately to a healthy organizational culture over the long term, sustainable and meaningful growth, and ongoing profit.

A VITAL SIGN OF CORPORATE HEALTH

If culture and leadership can have healing effects for an organization and its members, how then, do we know if a culture is sick? To begin with, if culture is toxic, the organization as a whole is not healthy; culture is a barometer of the health of an organization. The first thing I do in any situation is to simply observe how things are within an organization or team. It becomes obvious very quickly if there's a lot of suffering, toxicity, or disease, or if there is health. I pay attention to the way leaders interact, how communication flows, who gets to participate, and other subtle cues throughout the workplace.

I liken my consulting to that of a physician who is trained to diagnose, treat, and bring patients back to health. My

5   Ravinder Jit, C. S. Sharma, and Mona Kawatra, "Healing a Broken Spirit: Role of Servant Leadership," *Journal for Decision Makers* ,42(2) 80-94, 2017. Accessed on April 25, 2018, http://journals.sagepub.com/doi/pdf/10.1177/0256090917703754.

role is to diagnose, treat, and heal organizations, leaders, and teams. When I work with organizations, I spend time listening to how things operate. How do meetings happen? How do leaders interact? How do leaders create a space for others to be part of the meetings? Is there a lot of interruption? Is there widespread participation? Are people engaged? Are people fearful? Are they speaking up?

Subtle signals of the culture readily appear in the physical space within an organization as well. Pay attention to all the little nuances. How are offices distributed? Do people have access to executive spaces to talk with leaders, or is the space set up with barriers to prevent access? How an organization uses its space tells you a lot about its values and culture. Closed doors and drawn shades, for example, give you a pretty clear signal of secrecy.

Similarly, seeing how employees work can tell you a lot about the culture. Is there open space where people can have conversations, and shared space for collective work? Do people personalize their space with photos, etc., or is such personalization stifled? Can people bring part of their personal lives to work? Or is work very stiff with no one talking or collaborating?

One of the greatest signs of organizational health is often how administrative staff are treated within organizations. Are administrative staff treated as a core part of the team or as servants at the beck and call of the executive? At corporate events, how do individuals treat the wait staff? Simply observing those behaviors gives you a good idea of which actions are tolerated and which are rewarded in an organization. I once worked with a bank that required female employees to wear skirts and nylons. This dress code said a lot about their attitudes toward women in the workplace, and that attitude led to a lack of female representation in senior leadership and, I believe, to a resulting critical lack of market perspective.

There's a great saying that helps us understand an organization's culture: what you permit, you promote. As a physician of culture, I always look at what's permitted and promoted. Are the behaviors and actions in service of a love-based culture, or are they in service of fear, power, and control? In fear-based cultures, there's usually one person dominating the conversation. People blame each other, interrupt, criticize, and get defensive—all toxic behaviors that create fear and shut people down. Healthier organizations are much more participatory. Everyone gets an opportunity to share their opinions and voice their thoughts and perspectives. No one is shunned.

How leaders reward people and make decisions are also great indicators of culture. Is there intense competition with one winner and one loser? Are people rewarded at the expense of others? Are there incentives that lead to perverse behavior—unintended consequences that may harm another colleague or a different part of the organization? In better situations, are teams rewarded as a unit? Team rewards and recognition versus individual rewards and recognition are often indicators of overall health.

OTHER CHALLENGES TO CHANGING CULTURE

Why don't we see how healthy or unhealthy our own organizations are? We often become so accustomed to how things happen and how the culture operates that we don't see how it could be different. Oftentimes, as leaders, we have blinders on; we don't know what, if anything, is wrong or how to change it unless we take intentional steps to find out. There are resources that can help gauge what's working and what's not, such as cultural surveys that give you a sense of your strengths and blind spots. One survey I have found especially useful in today's world is the Denison culture survey. The Denison Model highlights strengths and weaknesses, highlights areas of internal friction, and captures key elements (adaptability, empowerment, vision, core values) that are essential to leading in today's world. You can review their survey through this link: https://www.denisonconsulting.com/culture-surveys/.

Culture is present every day, in every interaction, with every leader, in every part of the organization. No longer is culture just HR's job, though traditional organizations will often try to exile it here. In evolved organizations, HR is an instrumental partner for facilitating culture, but is no longer the sole owner of this work. Strengthening one's culture relies on the belief that culture is now everyone's job in the organization. Each individual is given the authority and responsibility to be good stewards of the desired culture. If the organization is moving to more transparency, the onus is on everyone to become aware of their behaviors and intentionally shift to more transparent practices. In this way, culture and operations cannot be separated.

Because leaders have a disproportionate impact on the overall culture, given their status and authority in most organizations, leadership development is an essential ingredient to strengthening the health of an organization's culture. As we saw in the introduction, only 58 percent of managers have any training before moving into a management position. As organizations evolve and release the beliefs and practices of our past, leaders need support in developing new practices to uplift the organization.

SOUL OF THE ORGANIZATION

As I summarize and close this chapter, I'll emphasize that culture is the soul of an organization. I believe evolved organizations will be identified by this human-centered approach, which will be seen and felt readily within an organization and outside of it by its customers, communities, partners, vendors, and investors. This soulfulness will not be something that organizations and leaders shy away from, but instead hold in deep regard for the goodness it brings to the world.

The following chapters highlight the practices and organizations that bring these concepts to life. I will provide insights into how we can operate from a place of love in action that allows for healing, well-being, purpose, and freedom.

Meaningful organizational change starts with culture.

CHAPTER SEVEN

Insights into Organizational Structure

Creating organizations of the future requires change on three interrelated levels: evolutionary leadership beliefs, organizational culture, and finally, organizational structure. When we talk about love in action, this is often where the rubber meets the road. Building meaningful structures and practices into how you operate is key to getting traction. The change is now and begins with you.

We know the vast majority of traditional change initiatives fail to create lasting change. We've discussed at length the management beliefs and practices that limit, or worse, sabotage our best efforts to foster meaningful change. However, I'm excited to be at this point with you. We are now equipped with a generative set of beliefs and leadership practices to pave the way for a different experience. This is the time for change, and I'm thrilled to highlight practices you can try today with your team and organization.

STARTING FRESH

You may be apprehensive about trying a new practice due to poor experiences in the past. However, I invite you to lean into the growth mindset and consider this as an experiment with no right or wrong outcome. No good or bad. It's simply a chance to try something new with your team. The key phrase here is "with your team." As you move through this chapter, think about how you can share your ideas with your colleagues and generate excitement or curiosity about a new way of working.

Don't think about massive sweeping changes. No longer can we map out a long-term change initiative with great clarity and predictable steps. Instead we must embrace a growth mindset focused on experimentation and iteration. What experiments are meaningful and safe to try with my team? What feedback loops do we need to put into place to gauge our progress? Framing change as an experiment allows us to iterate into the future in a much more dynamic and adaptable way.

Through this approach to change, we also rebuild trust that has eroded. Meaningful change begins with shared beliefs and conversations, continues through deliberate practice, and hinges on participation of all those who will be affected by the change—allowing them to experiment and create a way forward. Small, consistent actions of transparency and integrity need to happen over and over again to rebuild trust and credibility—it is a process that cannot be rushed. Slowly, over time, as these evolutionary beliefs and practices become solidified into the culture, people will respond with less and less skepticism, and over time, trust emerges.

INNOVATION CENTERS

I can best illustrate the potholes in the road to change through an example that often fails. Innovation centers are a popular trend right now in large organizations. The basic idea of an innovation center is a way for big organizations to carve out a small center where a group of employees can play with new ideas, be creative, and test change. This allows for a proving ground without having to change the entrenched bureaucracy organization-wide, or so the thinking goes. The problem is, innovation centers rarely work.

These centers, in practice, have not created the innovation leaders had hoped, leaving executives confused as to why and frustrated over the time and resources spent. The trouble is, no matter how much those in the Innovation Center are told to "be innovative, be creative," the underlying culture of the organization, often based in a fear-driven bureaucratic management system, stifles any progress. The lack of authority for those on the ground to make decisions, the inability to be autonomous, the organizational politics, and avoidance of risk strangles the life out of even the most well-intentioned people and ideas.

A better solution would be to first identify the barriers to innovation in the original organization. Culture has a unique way of embedding itself into what we might think of as new initiatives. Often, when looking retrospectively, we find that success requires leaders to let go of control and tolerate experiments and failure on the way to learning. People need to be allowed to play in the space of adaptability, try new ideas, move quickly and autonomously, fail quickly and fail big, and operate from a completely different culture. For most traditional organizations, tolerating the messiness and risk of this approach can feel like too much, and they inevitably go back to systems of command and control within a few years.

This is just one example of how organizations try to change but how the underlying beliefs of the organization continue to pervade. To get true innovation, you must make a change beyond just carving out space for creativity. You must shift your beliefs, practices, culture, and structure to allow change to emerge.

EXAMINING CORPORATE STRUCTURE

So how do we effect real, long-term change in practice? We must put all three elements to work—leadership beliefs, organizational culture, and structure. We've addressed the first two already. Now it's time to dive into structure. You can think of structure as how authority is distributed, how decisions are made, how departments are grouped, how people coordinate, as well as roles, responsibilities, and communication channels. Basic structure has an amazing way of creating behaviors. Be careful that it does so in ways you intend!

Leaders are the primary driver that allows structure to change. Leaders make a conscious choice of how power and authority are distributed, whether in traditional hierarchy or a flat, flexible structure that allows for more autonomy. Each choice has a distinct outcome. I've seen firsthand how the strict chains of command and control structures lead naturally to stifled creativity, innovation, and a culture of fear.

Structure drives behavior. Whenever we look at implementing a new practice or behavior in an organization, we also have to look at the underlying structures, driving it to get a better sense of what's going on. A structure that isolates people in silos tends to breed duplicated, uncoordinated work that is often wasted in the context of an organization's larger needs. A structure that is designed for collaboration, on the other hand, focuses on communication and coordination, even debate, but allows for more teamwork, perspectives, and robust work outcomes that meet challenges. If you want to shift a team's behavior from insulated and territorial to more collaborative and open, you need to focus change efforts at both the behavioral and structural levels. Ask questions: Are we creating constraints that hold people back from sharing their talents and potential with the organization? How can we remove those constraints to make cross-collaboration easy and natural? What structures can support the behaviors we want?

Most traditional organizations are structured in distinct silos or departments. The finance department doesn't talk to marketing or business development because they're all separate entities. They all have their own chains of command with no linkages between them. In a more flat or self-managed organization, the structure is different. These teams design work with purposeful integration between and across departments or functions. You may have heard of the terms "boundary spanner" or "lead link" to describe such a design. You might work in the finance department, but as a part of your role, you have an accountability to another department. As a lead link, you would be responsible for creating collaboration between the two departments, sharing information, and facilitating communication.

The different designs of these structures significantly impact the interactions of the teams. Having lead links or connections to other departments provides you an opportunity to gain insight into more information and different environmental factors, which allows a team to be more adaptable and responsive to the needs of the organization and market. This structural interconnection becomes the lifeblood of a team's health and effectiveness. Just like in the human body, when a part is completely isolated, it loses vitality and health, whereas the parts that are connected to the whole are fueled with blood, life, and oxygen to create vibrant health.

A BROADER PERSPECTIVE

We've seen how our outdated leadership beliefs can hold us back; our structures are no different. The org chart from the 1920s clearly highlights the fact that we have not evolved the design of our organizations to keep up with the needs of today's environment. Many of these structures limit our ability and capability to tap into the vast potential within the workforce and lack the nimbleness and adaptability we need to operate. I'd like to start by comparing three different structures to provide insight into the different possibilities that exist: a traditional hierarchy, a network of teams, and a self-managed organization.

TRADITIONAL HIERARCHY

Most of us have worked in an organization with a traditional hierarchy. In this structure, communication always flows from the top. Leaders create the strategy, make the decisions, and cascade the work, which more often than not leads to delays in work, disengagement, and lack of initiative. Innovation is quickly stifled by a need for control. Collaboration rarely exists, because everyone is operating in a vertical silo. Titles tend to play a more important role than knowledge, skills, or ability, and jobs are highly defined and constricted. Leadership often maintains power through fear-based tactics and lacks key feedback loops to gather real-time information from those closest to the work.

There are benefits to the traditional organization structure, however. It was born out of the need to create efficiency, and that is exactly what it achieves. Individuals are cogs in the wheel, doing a specific job over and over and over. In the modern landscape of constant change, however, mere efficiency is not enough. The limitations of traditional structure in the current environment quickly begin to outweigh its efficiency.

NETWORK OF TEAMS

Many would say the future of work will be played—and won—in teams. Organizational leaders are now beginning to experiment with team-based structures that allow for greater adaptability and innovation. One option for this is self-management, which may be considered too radical for many. Another option, occupying the middle ground, is a network of teams. We'll talk about this option first.

If you look closely into the operations of most organizations, work happens in small teams. Even if teams aren't formally created or recognized, work gets done through the collaboration (sometimes hidden collaboration) of a small group of people or network of people. The movement to shift toward a network of teams approach is based on the recognition of this natural tendency. Networks of teams form and disband swiftly based on the work that needs to get done and, as a result, meet often, share information freely, and collaborate with other teams as needed to achieve the goal.

In a network of teams structure, teams are set up almost as small entrepreneurial units. They are highly multi-disciplinary, which allows them to take on a variety of work where tasks are distributed based on talent and skills versus rigid job descriptions. Local teams are often responsible for day-to-day operations, including hiring, onboarding, marketing, sales, and profit and loss. Teams are given tremendous autonomy to operate in the way they see best.

A vividly clear sense of purpose provides the guidance and direction for teams to operate within the larger entity. However, these small teams often differentiate based on the specific objective they are trying to complete—like working with a specific client or fixing an issue within a product line. While their work is distinct, the shared purpose with the larger organization is what holds the teams together.

Lastly, members of the team will often nominate a colleague to function as a team leader or even choose to self-manage and achieve the work that needs to be completed. The typical boss with the title is replaced with a leader that is nominated by their peers with no requisite title or job description. The company Spotify is a great example of this type of structure. Their teams are called "squads," and each take responsibility for a unique part of the user experience. Interestingly, this structure also appears in the military. In the book *Team of Teams*, General Stanley McChrystal describes how the Joint Special Operations Task Force used decentralized authority in conjunction with highly trained and empowered teams to create a dynamic structure that allowed for greater flexibility, real-time information, and more accurate data.[1]

---

1   General Stanley McChrystal, *Team of Teams: New Rules of Engagement for a Complex World* (New York: Penguin Publishing Group, 2015).

Networks of teams have great flexibility to quickly adapt to market changes. Individuals are often on more than one team at a time, given the skills and passion they hold and what the organization needs. Individuals work on teams where they can make the most difference collaborating with the hierarchy removed. As a result, they are deeply engaged.

Leaders who are interested in moving from the traditional hierarchy to a structure with more freedom and autonomy tend to move in small steps. A leader might begin the journey by inviting three departments to work with additional autonomy and authority. Everyone then has the opportunity to experiment and then analyze the results to see how change might work practically within the organization.

These small tests of change give people a chance to see what works. The pitfall of this approach is the culture of the traditional organization or hierarchy tends to overrule the small experiments. Even with the intent to experiment with a different structure, leaders have to be exceptionally purposeful about giving away power and control to allow the experiment to be effective. With the right intention and work, however, this approach can overcome the pitfalls and go on to be highly successful.

Organizations can also choose a hybrid design that combines teams with hierarchy. Teams are empowered with distributed authority and decision-making, but the leadership structure remains to guide and coach. The more that local teams can be trusted and empowered, the more effective and adaptable the organization becomes. Any movement toward a network of teams is progress, even if it's accomplished partially and in small steps.

Upsides and Downsides

No structure is perfect, and the network of teams is no exception. Work in teams can be more challenging than heavily circumscribed bureaucracy and can require more of people.

A network of teams system challenges many of our long-standing leadership beliefs. To be effective in this structure, leaders have to give up control in favor of local autonomy. We must be self-confident enough to surround ourselves with smart people and willing to extend trust in the team to do what is best for the organization. Leaders must be able to set the expectation that we are all learning as we go. Failure becomes an opportunity to learn and do better next time. If leaders have the courage to let go of control and trust the team, this structure can be successful, but if we revert to the outdated beliefs of our past, the network of teams will never thrive.

This type of working environment is also demanding of

its team members. Individuals must have the internal motivation to be self-directed and take responsibility for problems or issues they see. In my experience, not everyone is ready and able to function in this capacity. Some individuals may lack the ability to work in a team or simply not want to be responsible and accountable for the work that needs to be done. Others honestly want people to tell them what to do.

Managing performance is also less straightforward in a team-centric organization. Ensuring things get done requires a much different mechanism. Rather than the manager's sole responsibility to make sure everything gets done—monitoring, tracking, reporting, etc.—it's now the responsibility of the entire team. Teams must establish procedures to track metrics collectively and implement practices to address performance issues amongst their peers.

While this may sound daunting, the advantages that come with this structure outweigh the disadvantages. Organizations reap significant benefits. Team members experience deeper engagement when they can utilize more of their talents and make more of the decisions impactful to their work. When given responsibility to align with changing market and organizational needs, people often display what is referred to as "organizational citizen behaviors," going above and beyond when they see a need. Individuals take responsibility to accomplish something outside of their formal job for the good of the team and organization. Often, this structure revitalizes the soul of organizations and individuals over time, releasing intrinsic motivation and joy. The results can be dramatic, both for organizations in terms of productivity and for the satisfaction and flourishing of the individuals themselves.

SELF-MANAGED ORGANIZATIONS

While self-managed organizations may seem radical to some, I've been fascinated by this structure since it caught my attention in *Reinventing Organizations* by Frederic Laloux. There have been several popular articles written about this movement, including *Harvard Business Review*'s "Let's Fire All the Managers,"[2] *Huffington Post*'s "The Age of the Self-Managed Organization,"[3] and several TED Talks by authors such as Doug Kirkpatrick,[4] just to name a few. Organizations adopting this structure are truly working on the cutting edge of the future of work.

What do we mean by a self-managed organization? Much

---

2   Gary Hamel, "First, Let's Fire all the Managers," *Harvard Business Review*, December 2011.

3   Great Work Cultures, "The Age of the Self-Managed Organization," Huffpost: The Blog, accessed April 28, 2018, https://www.huffingtonpost.com/great-work-cultures/the-age-of-the-selfmanage_b_6050162.html.

4   Doug Kirkpatrick, "Beyond Empowerment: Are We Ready for the Self-Managed Organization?" filmed November 2013 at TEDxChico, Chico, CA, video, 15:32, https://www.youtube.com/watch?v=Ej4n3w4kMa4.

has been written on this topic, and a Reinventing Organizations wiki site describes the major attributes best. In practice, these are the structures and processes most self-managed organizations adopt.

1. Autonomous teams—Rather than siloed workgroups, people come together in a network of interdependent small autonomous teams.
2. No bosses or org charts—Teams of the future let go of the need for a fixed hierarchy and rely on a more flat and self-directed approach to team leadership.
3. No job descriptions or titles—Rather, each individual adopts flexible roles that they define and commit to the team to fulfill.
4. Distributed decision-making—Anyone can make a decision as long as they get the advice from those the change affects.
5. Open information flow—All have access to the same information at the same time.
6. Participatory conflict resolution—Disagreements are resolved among peers through defined processes.[5]

Due to the need for transparency on a very large scale, the shift to this structure is often facilitated by a significant investment in technology. Technology is used to

5   "Self-Management," Reinventing Organizations Wiki: A Wiki to Inspire Next Generation Organizations, accessed April 26, 2018, http://www.reinventingorganizationswiki.com/ Self-Management.

enable a much greater flow of information, collaboration, and feedback for a team to continually refine their work and experiments.

Making the transition to self-management is a big leap for most organizations, but one many have chosen to do already. For examples, check out Morning Star, the world's leading tomato ingredients processor; Buurtzorg, a pioneering healthcare organization based in the Netherlands with a nurse-led model of holistic care; or W. L. Gore & Associate, best known for its Gore-Tex fabrics. All operate with a type of self-managed structure, celebrate the culture and soul of their organizations, and enjoy thriving businesses.

HIERARCHY IS NOT THE ISSUE

Should we fire all the bosses tomorrow? Perhaps not. Surprisingly, I don't have a problem with hierarchy. I think hierarchy can be used in a way that's effective and still allows for a love-based culture. Keeping a strongly hierarchical organization aligned with these evolutionary beliefs and practices requires constant feedback, experimentation, and adaptability from leaders. Power, control, and status are likely to sneak back into organization if leadership is not living in the practice of trust, guided by purpose, and oriented toward personal growth.

For a lot of leaders and organizations, no hierarchy is not

the answer. Being able to balance hierarchy with more love-based, purpose-driven, or human-driven practices may be the answer. To do this effectively, drive as much leadership and decision-making down to the local level as possible and allow individuals and teams to be an active part of how the organization operates. Be open and vulnerable as a leader, communicate frequently, and lead intentionally from a space of love.

Don't be afraid to embrace or modify the traditional or hybrid team structure if that's what works best for you and your organization. In some self-managed experiments, the chaos around the lack of structure, and at times wavering commitments to self-management, can create as much disadvantage as the stifling strictness of a traditional hierarchy. We call this the "tyranny of structurelessness."[6] When there are no guardrails and processes in place to guide a new way of working, people similarly don't thrive. It takes a committed leadership team and open and willing employees to work well in a self-managed environment.

Whatever answer makes the most sense for your organization, push the bounds of what you think is possible and lead to it deliberately. Keep an eye on structure, setting up the guardrails and processes to drive the behaviors you desire. Along the way, pay close attention to the beliefs

---

6   Jo Freeman, "The Tyranny of Structurelessness," JoFreeman.com, accessed April 28, 2018, http://www.jofreeman.com/joreen/tyranny.htm.

and culture; together, with the right structure and right practices, these will allow your organization to grow as healthy as possible over time.

CHAPTER EIGHT

Evolutionary Team Practices

As we've talked about before, structure plays a large role in organizational change. Meaningful, long-term behavioral change is immensely supported through aligned structural change. What, then, are the different organizational practices we can put into place that promote health in organizations and allow people's fullest potential and talent to come to life?

I recommend three key practices: one, moving away from a traditional job description and toward the ideas of roles. Two, moving away from the concentration of decision-making authority at the top of the organization to an advice process that provides active input and authority for anyone who senses a need for change. The final practice is building social agreements to ensure respect, honor, and accountability are in place for everyone on the team.

ROLES, NOT RIGID JOB DESCRIPTIONS

In traditional organizations, an absurd amount of time is wasted arguing about what to do, how to do it, and who should do it. Endless meetings are spent rehashing who is doing what by when. No one knows who has authority to decide on what issues and steps. No one is sure who is truly accountable for each decision, and no one wants to step outside of their rigid, static job description for concern of reprisal. These dynamics often promote learned helplessness and a general sense of apathy for the work at hand.

Instead of rigid job descriptions that lead to "not my job" mantras, role-based structures focus on one's talents and the needs of the organization. Roles are fluid and adaptable, meeting the needs of a changing world. I learned about the process of decoupling roles from souls as I studied Holacracy, a self-management structure for running purpose-driven, responsive organizations.

In the "roles not souls" framework, roles within an organization are separated from the people who are doing the work. This structure doesn't undermine the importance of people, but rather allows a team to look at what actual roles are needed to achieve their purpose. In a traditional job description, individuals have set accountabilities they need to accomplish based on the job they hold. If the needs of the organization shift and the job needs to change, there is a long process of reclassification to simply adjust the job description.

In this new framework, in contrast, one person may hold several different roles. Within each of the roles, there's a set of accountabilities that need to be accomplished. After roles have been clearly defined, individuals can attach to the work that is most meaningful. Organizations then open the potential of untapped talent within each member that may have been wasted outside of a typical job description. This also leads to amazing adaptability to change based on the needs of the organization, external market, and internal workforce needs.

The role-based structure is fundamentally different from traditional job descriptions in many ways. First, roles are based on an organizational purpose. This forces an organization to get clear about what roles are needed to achieve the desired purpose, what work those roles need to accomplish, and the authority given to each role. These questions are all about the role itself, not the people. Second, different people take on different roles at different times, and can grow into new roles and relinquish old ones according to reasonable rules that ensure the work gets done. Third, there's at least some distributed authority based on those roles. The person responsible for the role makes decisions applicable to that role. Finally, there are almost always more roles than employees, as individuals are often expected to select several roles that intersect with their unique skills and passions.

The real beauty of this design is the ease in which accountabilities can move from person to person without having to go through lengthy job reclassifications or even painful eliminations to create a new job. It is this adaptability that makes this design so powerful for organizations and so satisfying for individuals.

HOW IT WORKS

I've had the opportunity to experience a dynamic role-based organization directly, and to support teams in successful transitions from traditional jobs to more adaptable roles. The first step is to diligently move through a role identification process. There are two distinct processes I'd recommend. The first is to identify each of the roles that must happen on a daily basis to get the work of the organization done. With a preliminary list in hand, begin to write the specifics for each role, including its purpose, responsibilities, and accountabilities based on the collective wisdom of all in the group. Percolab, an organization based out of Canada, France, and Belgium, has a fantastic process that I've used with success. For their in-depth, step by step approach, take a look at their article here: http://www.percolab.com/en/self-management-roles-and-process-design/.

The second process you can use to identify roles is to begin from scratch at the ground level and identify all the accountabilities—all of the ongoing activities that need to be done—first. Then group the like accountabilities together, focusing on the nature of the work, not who is doing it now. Each grouping can then be labeled with a specific role by cluster or category. This process is often recommended by Holacracy practitioners, and there's a useful guide you can use at this link: https://medium.com/@Energized/getting-started-with-holacracy-4-tips-to-define-a-first-set-of-roles-and-accountabilities-f3c5c22cbc4a.

There's no recipe for role identification that fits all situations, so it's important to keep an open mind and work on creative solutions for your individual needs. The best solutions are often those that are hacked from several different approaches to meet the unique needs of the team. Building roles can be time intensive, but provides great value in increased adaptability and autonomy. With a role-based structure, anyone can propose a change to a role at any time by simply calling for a brief team meeting, sharing a proposal, and gaining approval. Adjustments are made in real time as the needs of the teams and individuals evolve.

Moving away from rigid job descriptions to a more fluid, organic process gives individuals the ability to create roles that exemplify their own strengths. When individuals work from their strengths, the organization wins, and individuals win as well, as they now have the freedom and authority to articulate how they want to contribute to a shared purpose. They are free to identify needs and fill them, participating in something much larger than themselves. This is an ideal example of love in action—providing individuals the freedom to experience their own power and capacity to create their world.

ROLES AND NEW CONVERSATIONS

A role-based organizational design will naturally elicit new and different types of conversations—some which may be awkward to manage initially. Let's take an example. A team is faced with a specific role or maybe even a set of roles that need to get done, but no one has interest in doing them. What happens now? This creates an incredible opportunity for a conversation about priorities and needs. Why is there no interest in taking on this role? Is the role even needed? Does it provide the team and organization value? The result of this conversation may require the team to hire additional individuals who do have an interest in accomplishing this role, or possibly dissolving the role completely. The point here is that it becomes a team conversation about what needs to be done to achieve the shared purpose.

Teams most often divvy up roles based on what feels fair and equitable given the amount of time dedicated to their work (full-time workers hold more roles than individuals working part-time.) Sometimes there becomes a perceived imbalance, however. In a situation where it feels like someone isn't pulling their weight or not doing as much as other team members, it becomes the responsibility and authority of the team members to call a meeting and discuss the situation. With a specific issue at hand, any team member can call a meeting and voice a concern and say, "Heather's not pulling her weight. She has three roles. I have seven. We work the same hours, and I'm feeling completely overworked. We have to do something different." Then it becomes a conversation for the team to hash out. Maybe Heather is suffering because her life at home is imploding and she needs to go part time for a while. Maybe she's no longer a great fit for the organization and doesn't have a desire to be there doing the work. Maybe the team just needs clarity and for Heather to say, "I'm doing three roles, but they actually require this amount of work and this amount of time based on the projects within these roles." When everyone can have a transparent conversation around all the variables, often the issue can be resolved in a way that feels true to everyone's needs.

In a more formal, traditional hierarchy, when someone isn't pulling his or her weight, it's normal for someone on the team to go to the boss and complain. In those circumstances, the boss may know about Heather's struggles with her responsibilities at home but be unable to talk about them publicly, or may not do anything to resolve the issue at hand. Without this transparency, the lack of conversation breeds resentment and frustration. With full engagement and transparency, the team as a whole can work together to resolve difficult circumstances in a useful way. These conversations are new and different from what we are used to in traditional organizations, but they are an important part of growing into love in action, both as individuals and organizations. By being willing to have hard conversations, we embrace the process of evolution and move into the future of work.

IMPACT ON RECRUITING

In organizations that have moved to a role-based structure, an interesting dynamic often arises. Individuals who leave to take a different job at another organization realize they can't work in a traditional structure anymore and return. They realize the wholeness that results from working in a role-based structure and want to be engaged and fulfilled in that way.

This structure provides the essential ingredients of intrinsic motivation—purpose, autonomy, and mastery—that Dan Pink calls for in his book *Drive*.[1] Team members are aligned to a shared purpose, have the autonomy to select roles that best fit their strengths, and the ability to build new skills that will progress their growth and career.

Because of this dynamic, a role-based system often provides a long-term competitive advantage in recruiting and retention. News travels fast when people love what they do and are excited to share new opportunities to experience a new way of working. The organization becomes a magnet for great talent.

NO MORE "THAT'S NOT MY JOB"

We've all heard the frustrating workplace comment, "That's not my job." When you move toward a role-based system, the "that's not my job" excuse become a nonissue or clearly highlights an individual who does not fit well in this type of structure. A rigid job description creates a very clear demarcation about what your job is and is not. When you move to a role-based system, that demarcation

---

[1] Daniel H. Pink, *Drive: The Surprising Truth about What Motivates Us* (New York: Riverhead Books, 2011).

dissolves as you can choose to take on a new role or to give one up. If there's a role that needs to be done within the organization that no one is doing, then the team has the opportunity to explore the value of the role in achieving the goals and take the appropriate next steps. A role-based system, then, becomes a tool for accountability and progress. Responsibility cuts both ways.

THE ADVICE PROCESS

Let's move to our next practice. The ability to make quick and effective decisions at work is a critical skill for leaders and employees across an organization. However, this can also be a source of significant frustration and wasted time when done poorly. As such, many evolved organizations are exploring new processes with which to make decisions, and one great place to begin is what's called the "advice process." The term was coined by Dennis Bakke, who used the practice extensively in his own organization and wrote a book about it called *The Decision Maker*.[2]

Bakke says, "Few leaders tap into the value created by putting important decisions in the hands of their people. Instead, "team players" are taught to do what they're told. This takes the fun out of work. And it robs people of the chance to contribute in a meaningful way. Or organiza-

---

2   Dennis Bakke, *The Decision Maker: Unlock the Potential of Everyone in Your Organization, One Decision at a Time* (Seattle, WA: Pear Press, 2013).

tions will use a participatory style of decision-making in which recommendations are given to the boss, who then makes the final decisions. This approach also fails to fully realize the value of the people in the organization."[3] To fully empower our people and operate with love in action, we must provide opportunities to contribute in meaningful ways, including decision-making. This, Bakke says, is why something like the advice process is so powerful.

For any leader who feels anxious about decisions being made haphazardly, don't be alarmed—there are checks and balances in place to ensure sound decisions happen. The advice process bakes the checks and balances into the practice itself, while ensuring decisions are made at a local level by those who know the information best. There are several ways to design an advice process. For example, some leaders will decide as long as the individual follows the agreed upon process, touches base with everyone impacted by the problem, and gets a decision approved by the team, they can go forward and make any decision on the local level. Other leaders create guardrails around what decisions can be made based on the role you occupy. For example, if an individual has taken on a role in the finance area and is in charge of getting financial reports compiled on a monthly basis, she has financial decision-making authority based on that specific role.

---

3   Bakke, *The Decision Maker*, 10.

Distributed decision-making can coexist with a hierarchy. However, the role of leadership changes in this dynamic to that of a coach. Once this authority is distributed, leaders support the process, provide guidance and coaching as needed, and only intervene when absolutely necessary. When the team hits a stalemate between two different perspectives, the leader can step in and help move the process along. This can be a challenging transition for leaders, but one that is also rewarding as you witness the growth and development of the team members all around.

To give you a basic perspective on an alternative approach for decision-making, I'll share simple instructions on how I've used the advice process in action and how I've seen it used effectively in organizations. However, for full instruction on the advice process, check out *The Decision Maker*.

There are four basic steps.

STEP ONE: SENSING AN ISSUE

The first step is sensing an issue or tension in the work environment. The dynamic is not a manager coming in and saying, "We have a problem. You need to fix it." No, the team or individual member notices a problem and brings it to the team to get addressed and resolved. This first step requires an open and ongoing invitation for team members to take this initiative and carve out time to address issues as they arise.

STEP TWO: GATHERING INPUT

After the individual identifies a problem, it is their responsibility to gather information, perspectives, and opinions regarding the matter from those affected by the situation or from those who have specific and relevant expertise.

STEP THREE: CRAFTING A PROPOSAL

After gathering all the input from those closest to and most knowledgeable about the issue, the individual who identified the problem drafts a proposal and shares it with the team.

The proposal spells out a specific solution to the problem and can take any action based on the issue or tension. For example, a tension may arise related to frequent absenteeism on a team. In this case, a policy would be drafted for the team to agree to review, revise, and approve. Another issue could be ongoing bugs in a software product. In that case, the individual who senses the problem might create a technical proposal to repair the product and prevent future ongoing quality issues. Different problems require different kinds of proposals, but the proposal should always be clear and specific with a solution to the problem at hand.

Once everyone has had a chance to review the proposal, the team as a whole then discusses, reviews, refines, and comes to an approved solution.

STEP FOUR: ACTION

After taking the team's advice into account, the individual decides on an action or commitment to be done and communicates it to all concerned. The individual's responsibility is to ensure that the change is documented and well understood by those it impacts.

It's important to remember all the steps are driven at the local level. Anyone on the team can identify or sense a problem or tension, and is then responsible for gathering input, creating the proposal, reviewing it, incorporating changes with the team, then driving the action. The decision-maker—the one who senses the problem and who is often not the formal leader—seeks advice from their peers, then makes the decision. With a more formal hierarchy in place, the process may require consultation at different levels within the organization, up to the Board, if needed, based on the issue. The biggest difference from most traditional structures are clear: the problem is not simply sent to the boss to handle. The team handles the issue themselves.

SPECIFICS OF THE ADVICE PROCESS

There are some important principles to follow as part of this process. First, the decision-maker who senses the problem must always seek advice. They cannot go all the way to an action or a conclusion without talking to those who it affects. Second, the bigger the problem, the more people need to be involved, from those affected to those who have the knowledge to those externally who are impacted.

Third, while it's empowering to be able to make decisions, the responsibility also follows. The decision-maker bears the responsibility to carry out the advice process from start to finish and to ultimately make the decision as a result. Notably, the collective is responsible for the outcome of the decision, but it's the individual who must shepherd the decision through the process. Carrying this kind of responsibility might sound daunting, but is an exceptional opportunity for everyone to learn and grow.

The advice process has incredible benefits for leaders and organizations who take it on. One, the process creates a sense of community. By seeking advice and convening conversations, all of those around you get to be a part of the team formed to solve the pressing issue. Two, this process fosters a sense of humility. We all know at times asking for advice can be hard, but it's exactly what this process requires. It forces individuals to tap into others for information and ask for help to create a viable solution.

Three, this process focuses on and facilitates a growth mindset. Learning from the impact of your decisions is incredible on-the-job education. You must be able to embrace the idea that you might fail and that everyone will learn together from the outcome.

Fourth, Bakke says that this process creates better decisions. By distributing the authority to those closest to the issue, stronger and better-informed decisions result. The advice process, or any practice that decentralizes authority to the local team, exemplifies trust and autonomy, which are both needed for the evolution of organizations and leaders.

THE PRACTICE OF SOCIAL AGREEMENTS

In line with creating a culture that is based on caring human connections, the absence of fear, and the freedom and autonomy to design your work, social agreements become a key tool in your leadership toolkit.

You can think of social agreements as the commitments you make with one another about what work needs to get done as well as how you intend to work together. These commitments are not a set of policies, or a copy-and-pasted version of the organization's core values, but rather a dynamic set of mutual expectations that are cocreated, reviewed regularly, and revised often at a team level. They can be as simple as a list or as elaborate as a visual diagram, wiki page, or video montage. Be as creative as you like as you go through this process in a way meaningful to your individual team.

The real purpose of creating a social agreement within a team is to allow expectations, explicit as well as implicit, to come to life. What expectations do you have around the work that needs to get done, and how do you intend to engage with one another on the team? What is working well within the team? What is not? What should the team keep doing, start doing, or stop doing to ensure it's performing at the level it desires?

Unfortunately, some of the most toxic work environments happen when teams are filled with disrespect and unmet commitments. There is a violation of an implicit contract or agreement about how we treat one another. According to *Firms of Endearment*,[4] an organization's stakeholders are often bound by two different types of implicit social contracts: one on the emotional/interpersonal level and the other on a transactional/legal level. The emotional level deals with all the intangible and qualitative, hard-to-measure elements related to how we work—how our values, purpose, passions, and talents, as well as our social interactions or feelings of safety and trust are met in the workplace. In other words, the emotional level is about

---

4   Sisodia, Sheth, and Wolfe, *Firms of Endearment*, 62.

being human, how we are treated, and how we show up emotionally at work. The transactional level, in contrast, deals with tangible elements such as performance criteria and the explicit goals employees are asked to meet or complete.

By having an explicit social agreement, it's much easier to have clear expectations, to deal with conflict quickly, and to create an open team environment where members feel safe and empowered.

THREE KEY DISTINCTIONS

There are three additional key distinctions that need to be understood as you move into the process of building social agreements.

The first is accountability. A social agreement requires a team to determine up front how to handle violations. If you have a stated element in your social agreement that says you are all going to show up on time to all meetings, what happens if someone doesn't show up on time? How is that violation handled?

The second is team buy in. A social agreement can't be mandated by a leader or a manager. It loses effectiveness when someone says, "This is how you have to show up at work." A social agreement also can't be created effectively if only half the team is interested in creating it. The beauty and essence of this process is in the cocreation of the agreements as well as the outcomes. If a member or members of the team don't wish to participate, it can be challenging. To get the most benefit, each member must sincerely care about the success of the team and each other for the process to make a difference.

If full team engagement is not possible, simply do your best. As a team, you can move through the process, get as much input as possible, and experiment until you find an agreement that works. I find more often than not, peer pressure plays a huge role in team performance and dynamics. If the majority of the team is operating in a certain way, the few members who are resistant will either come along with the change over time or self-select out.

Third is the flexibility to evolve the agreement as needed. A social agreement is not meant to be painted on the wall or printed in a brochure. When I went through the process of creating a new social agreement with a client, after a week we were ready for its first revision. Instead of creating rigidity around core values that are thought of as stable and enduring, there is tremendous freedom in knowing a social agreement can and should change. Being in a continuous open and honest conversation about how you intend to be in a relationship at work is a liberating experience and allows for great experimentation and iteration.

A social agreement is where the magic happens. It's where people come together and collectively decide how to be in a relationship together at work. It's a birthplace of trust, commitment, ownership, and innovation. It drives the creation process back to the employees versus a leader or manager having to tell someone how they have to be at work.

When people get to be a part of the creative process, it results in greater performance, greater engagement, and better results.

Each of these practices highlight love in action at work. They also outline the shift in the role of a leader from that as an authoritarian to a servant and coach in pursuit of a shared purpose. Organizations of the future will rely on these structures and practices to fuel their success by tapping into the depths of talent, motivation, and passion that traditional organizations squelch.

CHAPTER NINE

Dare to Be Different

EVOLVED ORGANIZATION
CASE STUDIES

In this chapter, I am excited to share several case studies from organizations that are true inspirations. They have courageously built practices that exemplify love in action and challenge the status quo. In the following chapter, I'll highlight how these evolutionary steps not only make a meaningful difference for business outcomes but also affect the well-being of all those the business touches.

The future of work will depend on these organizations' and leaders' willingness to boldly pave a new path for others to follow. As the saying goes, with risk comes reward. These early adopters are, in many ways, carrying the risk for those leaders who stand aside watching to see what might result. Fortunately, as we've previously discussed, we are finding more and more data to suggest they are on the right path. Many of these evolved organizations are outperforming traditional organizations by ratios of 8:1. Those businesses who can adopt more humanistic practices and continue to iterate will be the ones that not only survive, but thrive in this new, demanding, rapidly changing age of work. We look to these early adopters to show us the way.

In the following pages, I will highlight four different case studies: Decurion, Scribe, August, and Percolab. My intention is to provide a variety of examples and possibilities for you to study as you think about how your organization can evolve to meet the challenges you face. Reflect on these examples and notice what practices excite and intrigue you. Those insights may, in fact, reveal the best place for you to start on this journey. I'll note here that none of these organizations are my clients, nor am I being paid to share their stories and examples.

Let's begin.

THE DECURION CORPORATION

Decurion, based in California, is an organization that has been a true inspiration. I was first introduced to their work in the book *An Everyone Culture: Becoming a Deliberately*

Developmental Organization.[1] Since then, I have had the great pleasure of speaking with their Chief Purpose Officer, Bryan Ungard, to better understand the inner workings of these practices.

Decurion's purpose, their fundamental reason to exist, is to provide places for people to flourish. They believe every human being has something unique to express in the world, and they work to create the conditions on an organizational level in which that expression will emerge. Their emphasis on being human at work combined with creating value through business excellence truly sets their business model apart.

Interestingly, reading Decurion's purpose statement doesn't give you a clear sense of what business they operate. That is intentional. As the business grows in a variety of directions, they focus on one central theme—an unwavering dedication to providing places for people to flourish and businesses that flourish. Decurion operates Pacific Theaters, ArcLight Cinemas, and Robertson Properties Group, one of the leading real estate development and property management companies in Southern California. They've also recently added Hollybrook Senior Living, which extends their purpose by creating environments for seniors to flourish, a much-needed addition to the

1   Robert Kegan and Lisa Laskow Lahey, *An Everyone Culture: Becoming a Deliberately Developmental Organization* (Boston: Harvard Business School Publishing, 2016).

healthcare industry. In each part of their business, Decurion works to grow and expand their human development practices as well as business outcomes. These two seemingly separate goals become one overarching purpose.

Decurion is deeply intentional and committed to creating this unique way of being and organizational culture. In fact, they've been on this journey for the last fifteen years. Christopher Forman, Decurion CEO, says, "For us, pursuing profitability in human development emerges as one thing. We do not see a tradeoff... The moment we consider sacrificing one for the other, we recognize we have lost both."[2] The organization has married people development with profitability and has seen that, by working in conjunction, all thrive exponentially.

A DELIBERATELY DEVELOPMENTAL ORGANIZATION

Decurion is one example of a new breed of evolved organizations, what's called a Deliberately Developmental Organization (DDO). "A DDO is a culture that is organized around the simple but radical conviction that organizations will best prosper when they are more deeply aligned with people's strongest motive, which is to grow."[3] It's a

2   Kegan and Lahey, *An Everyone Culture*, 186.

3   "An Everyone Culture: Becoming a Deliberately Developmental Organization," book description, *Harvard Business Review*, accessed April 28, 2018, https://hbr.org/product/ an-everyone-culture-becoming-a-deliberately-developmental-organization/14259-HBK-ENG.

concept well worth a deep dive for any leader desiring to create a different experience of work. As Kegan and Lahey point out so eloquently, "DDO work settings are built for human development. They support people in overcoming their limitations as part of contributing to the profitability of the business. It's just as true that DDOs seek profitability so that they can stay in business to help people overcome their limitations and grow."[4] The DDO model embraces evolution and love in action, and I would encourage you to do more research on the topic beginning with Kegan and Lahey's book *An Everyone Culture*. You may find the path is perfect for your organization.

DECURION PRACTICES

I'm going to share two specific practices within Decurion that allow this unique model and culture to come to life. However, before we dive in, it is important to note that while the organization focuses on human development and flourishing, that does not necessarily equate to a focus on happiness. Decurion's Chief Purpose Officer, Bryan Ungard, explains,

> When people hear 'flourishing' they think of appreci-ation and good feelings. But growth and development does not always equal 'feeling good.' Our culture is not about maximizing the minutes you feel good at

---

4   Kegan and Lahey, *An Everyone Culture*, 13.

work. We don't define flourishing by sitting-around-the-campfire moments. We ask people to do seemingly impossible things."[5]

Love is not necessarily easy and comfortable and is often tough. Love pushes us to our edges.

Check-Ins

At Decurion, they begin their meetings with a process called a "check-in." By checking in, individuals "say whatever they need to [in order] to bring themselves fully, as whole people, into the work space."[6] This seemingly simple practice has deep implications for how people come together. It is a warm welcome for your whole person at work, and a key practice that translates Decurion's values directly into the everyday workday.

The process is quite simple. At the start of a meeting, an invitation is opened for people to check in and share whatever is on their minds. Speaking up is voluntary; people can pass with no obligation. Often, individuals share whatever they need to bring themselves fully to the present. In check-ins which I've participated in, I might share how I am feeling about the meeting at hand, my frustration about a work or life situation that I need to let

---

5   Kegan and Lahey, *An Everyone Culture*, 35.

6   Kegan and Lahey, *An Everyone Culture*, 28.

go of to be present, or a simple reflection of something fun I did last night. The beauty of this is found in its organic nature. Nothing is scripted or should be.

When I suggest this exercise to leaders I'm working with, I am often told it's a waste of time. They ask, "Why are we spending half an hour checking in before this meeting when we know we just need to get to X, Y, and Z?" However, bringing humanity back to work and valuing someone's wholeness allows people to show up with whole hearts. Taking the time to ask what's on everyone's mind and heart before we dive into business fosters real engagement and creates vulnerability for people to develop trust and lasting relationships.

You also get to know people on a much more human level through these exchanges—even if it's from one statement at a check in. A single comment could connect you and that individual forever. I recall being in a meeting with a group of strangers and going through a rather vulnerable check in, which lasted close to forty-five minutes. One individual shared a story that resonated deeply and truly connected us through a common experience. This connection would have never surfaced otherwise, and our working relationship was immediately crystalized through a shared experience. Check-ins are incredible practice grounds for vulnerability and courage. What seems like a really simple practice is deeply powerful, human, and personal.

LEARNING COMMUNITY

Everything within the Decurion organization is built on the structure they call learning community. The organization is still privately held with a hierarchy of leaders, but members of the organization participate in "communal governance structures,"[7] similar to what was described previously as a network of teams. These communities, such as within the theater group or the real estate division, provide the fertile ground for deep personal learning, and improve decision-making for the organization overall. Decurion has said that learning community is a critical part of their success, and is a perfect example of the growth mindset in operation.

Learning communities don't replace hierarchies for Decurion—they have an integrated approach, as they believe there is a strong role for hierarchy. However, the learning community has the primary responsibility for the success of the business. Even if leaders are held accountable in the end, everyone speaks, everyone contributes and everyone is responsible for the communities' outcomes. All team members are expected to step up, spot problems, and take the initiative to move the organization forward.

One key element of Decurion's learning community is their ability to embrace differences and diversity. We often think about diversity as a problem and something we have

---

7   Kegan and Lahey, *An Everyone Culture*, 36.

to create strategies to address. Decurion sees diversity as something to embrace. They partner with people to enhance diversity and allow them to work through the challenges that arise when they come together from different worldviews.

These communities are created by engaging in a set of guidelines and practicing the "principles of community." The principles of community include:

- Communicate with authenticity
- Deal with difficult issues
- Welcome and affirm diversity
- Relate with integrity and respect
- Balance holding on and letting go
- Tolerate ambiguity and learning anxiety

The guidelines include:

- Use "I" statements but don't generalize
- We are equally responsible
- We respect confidentiality
- Include yourself and others equally[8]

What does it take to build a learning community?

---

8   "Building Learning Communities," Decurion Corporation Blog, accessed April 28, 2018, http://www.decurion.com/dec/building-learning-communities/.

MOVING TO A LEARNING COMMUNITY

Moving from a traditional structure to this type of community requires a thoughtful change approach and realistic expectations. Decurion shares the four stages introduced by Dr. M. Scott Peck in his book *A Different Drum* that teams move through when shifting from a conventional group to a learning community.[9] The first stage is what they call a pseudo community. This is the most common way that most work groups function in traditional organizations. Colleagues come together for requisite meetings, speak in generalities, don't look for differing perspectives and opinions that might deepen the conversation and enrich the outcome, and generally avoid deeper exploration. Conflict is to be avoided and most will practice good manners. Unfortunately, there's no fundamental progress in this stage.

Next, an evolving team goes through a stage of chaos where differences begin to emerge. The group begins to see and try to deal with unresolved issues. There is a lot of talk, but very little listening. Groups, struggling with the chaos and conflict, often attempt to force resolution by looking to a leader to solve the issue at hand—the traditional approach to most decision-making. In this stage, teams will also attempt to escape the discomfort by forming subcommittees to resolve the conflict or dismiss

---

9   M. Scott Peck, *The Different Drum: Community Making and Peace* (New York: Touchstone, 1987).

it completely. We see these maneuvers all the time in the command-and-control structures.

The third stage teams must go through is a space of emptying. This is very similar to the trust mindset discussed in Chapter 4. We must let go of our expectations, preconceptions, solutions, the need to be in control, and the need to know. There is a sense of surrender as we let go of what we feel is right and instead follow the group as it moves through the process. This doesn't mean withdrawing in times of frustration, but literally letting go of our need to control and instead participate in the process of learning together. This is when true listening enters back into the team environment.

By going through the emptying process, communities can move to the final stage, what Decurion calls learning community. Here, individuals can move beyond the reactive ego and experience an openness and curiosity to others' opinions and perspectives. Differences are acknowledged and honored. The team moves from conflict avoiding to conflict resolving. Colleagues can debate and argue effectively without being disrespectful or taking comments personally.[10]

---

10   Kegan and Lahey, *An Everyone Culture*, 36.

LOVE IN ACTION AT DECURION

I am hoping by this time in the book, you can see that the "soft" stuff is key to building Evolved Executives and evolved organizations. We don't have to trade profits for a more caring and human workplace. We don't have to neglect business outcomes to achieve personal growth and development. The two can happen simultaneously, and the "soft" stuff often actively supports profit. "We see a big difference in our revenues and experience of our guests because we focus on people's development and their critical thinking. What's right for the business actually creates meaning and confidence for the crew members. We've had breakthrough results in every category. This is not just fun and games."[11]

Decurion's focus on human flourishing creates meaningful business results critical to the organization's success.

SCRIBE MEDIA

Scribe is another amazing organization to check out, one that is practicing love in action from a very evolved and practical perspective. I came across Scribe as I was searching for people- and purpose-focused organizations that are exceptionally successful in the marketplace.

The Scribe mission is to unlock the world's wisdom. The

---

11   Kegan and Lahey, *An Everyone Culture*, 196.

organization believes human culture advances through people sharing their ideas, knowledge, and wisdom with each other. The recording and sharing of knowledge, especially through books, has been at the root of all human progress. The problem, however, is that it's often hard for busy people to write books.

Scribe has thrown the book writing process on its head. They have created a seamless system for the book creation process that allows you to quickly move from idea to published work. Their structured process involves working with authors first to create a tight and professional outline to lay the foundation of the book; then interviewing the authors to gather all the insights, stories, and knowledge needed for the books; and finally, in collaboration with the authors, turning these transcripts into beautifully written manuscripts.

Beyond the obvious innovative approach to the process of book creation, the organization has crafted several evolved internal practices that are worth sharing. As I've mentioned previously, many organizations struggle with values that are words without actions. Evolved organizations find ways to breathe life into their values and ensure they guide the organization through purposeful business growth. Scribe does this well.

Scribe has core values that are central to their operations and culture. The unique and exceptionally powerful element to these ten values is that each have a distinct opposite or antithesis. A good core value is one that has a clear definition and behavioral example. However, a great core value is one that people can understand by seeing what the opposite would look or feel like. When values have this articulated tension, team members can easily understand the organizational expectation of how to behave and what to prioritize. Scribe does this eloquently.

Scribe's values are listed below.

- Principle 1: We before me.
  - Opposite: You're only out for yourself, no one else.
- Principle 2: Bring your whole self to work.
  - Opposite: Keep business and personal separate.
- Principle 3: We all eat the same dirt.
  - Opposite: People treated differently according to their rank.
- Principle 4: Tell your tribe the truth.
  - Opposite: Don't speak up, just be quiet, or keep it to smaller groups.
- Principle 5: The glass is already broken.
  - Opposite: If it ain't broke, don't fix it.
- Principle 6: Ask questions.

- ◦ Opposite: Do things the way we've always done them.
- Principle 7: Shoot the message, never the messenger.
  - ◦ Opposite: Judge people harshly if you don't like their ideas.
- Principle 8: Act like an owner.
  - ◦ Opposite: Just do what you're told.
- Principle 9: Culture fits always have their place.
  - ◦ Opposite: People rise to the level of their incompetence.
- Principle 10: Do right by people.
  - ◦ Opposite: Rules dictate action.[12]

These principles are powerful for the organization and employees because they give a clear description of day-to-day behaviors. The expectations are clear. It becomes obvious when there is a violation of stated values.

This is a type of social agreement on an organizational level. The principle of "tell your tribe the truth" is a massive social agreement in contrast to the norm in most organizations, "Don't speak up or only speak when spoken to." I asked cofounder Tucker Max what happens in a gossip situation. He explained that if someone comes to you to talk about someone else, you simply say, "Hey, have you talked to that individual already about the issue?"

---

12 The Scribe Culture Doc, public working draft, accessed May 10, 2018, https://docs.google.com/document/d/1cqXRwrk1fYuFTglAR3lpu94egZDfXN_M12qVX_t1ev8/edit.

If the answer is no, the right answer is then to say, "Part of our values is you need to tell the truth. You don't need to speak behind their back. I need you to go and talk to that individual before you talk to me." Articulating these specific behaviors gives the values meaning and clarity. Everyone knows the expectations and how best to show up at work.

Beyond striving to create an internal culture that is human-focused, Scribe also strives to do the same with their freelance workforce. Their goal is to be the "best gig in the gig economy." Many of us know the gig economy is not always pretty. Freelancers, oftentimes, are treated as cheap labor and asked to work more for less pay and benefits. Scribe celebrates freelancers as an integral part of their success and sees an opportunity to set a high standard for caring for and valuing freelancers. They proceed from a culture of abundance, firm in their belief that generous behaviors lead to success for all—the organization as well as the freelancer.

THE WHOLE SELF PROGRAM

All of this made me dig a little deeper into the organization, and I found another incredible practice at Scribe embodying love in action: the whole self program. I encourage you to sincerely consider how to take a program like this and make it your own.

The Whole Self Program begins with something they call the strength and obstacles exercise. Every six months, the team organizes an off-site for employees and uses this opportunity to dive into personal growth and development. With the entire group sitting in a circle, one individual (usually a newer member of the team) becomes the focus of the conversation. What ensues is a deep and rich reflection on that individual's strengths and obstacles on a very authentic level. The reflection starts with strengths. Every team member takes a turn to describe what they see as that individual's true strengths, the things they do really well, with specific examples and stories. Oftentimes, the individual walks away with thirty to forty specific items and stories, and they're blown away. For many, it's the first time they've heard a group of people lavishly praise them.

Next, the individual has the chance to share with the larger team what he or she wants to accomplish in the next year—this doesn't necessarily need to be specific to work, but could be anything in their life that matters to them. It could be self-development, relationships, or whatever is relevant to them personally. That individual is asked to dive in and think about what the goal looks and feels like, then share that with the entire group. I imagine this is an inspiring conversation to experience and a bit overwhelming for the individual in the spotlight.

After the individual shares their goals, the conversation

moves to obstacles. The team begins to describe the items they see blocking the individual's ability to achieve the goal, the attributes the person needs to work on in themselves to be successful. It's important for the individual to hear these from an objective, outside perspective, in a supportive, caring, nurturing way. Individuals walk away with a concrete list of items to improve upon to achieve their goal.

At the end of the off-site, the individual who went through the strengths and obstacles exercise picks someone within the tribe to act as their guide. They meet once a month until the next summit to work on the specific goal and create a plan to get there. Team members of Scribe found this exercise so valuable they asked for this mentorship more frequently, which is when the Whole Self Program became part of the fabric of Scribe's everyday practices and culture.

Similar to DDOs, this organization truly invests in the development of the whole person. Scribe believes investing in humans is in the best interest of the organization. It takes a huge degree of investment from a leadership perspective to create a space where people can show up as wholly and fully as possible, but the results are powerful. Practices like these heal each of us, create healthier organizations, and lead to meaningful business outcomes.

APPLYING SIMILAR PRACTICES

You can apply these ideas to your own situation in several ways. First, reflect on how you as a leader view people development in your organization. Do you view it as nice to have, as something HR does, or as an integral part of your business strategy? What is your role as a leader in cultivating people development? What do you want it to be?

I'll never advocate you take on another's practice wholesale and simply apply it in a cookie-cutter way to your unique situation. That being said, looking at what other successful businesses are doing can give you practical ideas to adapt and implement. If you hold the core belief that human development is a cornerstone of your strategy, Scribe gives you a quick glance into a practice that could be implemented on many different scales, as Decurion did above. Consider, how can I ensure individuals are having conversations around their strengths, what they want to accomplish, and their obstacles? How can I use others in the organization as coaches or guides to help individuals evolve and grow? Then you can examine the beliefs and practices you can bring into the organization to move it in this direction. Have fun creating something unique to you and your organization, and don't be afraid to experiment and to learn by iteration.

AUGUST

Radical transparency is a theme that is emerging more and more in popular articles and books, and I am excited by the increased attention. Many organizations have taken notable steps to increase transparency. As a leader, you may already share financial reports with every member of your team and the organization as a whole. You may post customer satisfaction and employee engagement scores publicly for people to review as they wish. However, few have taken the bold step to share pay transparently! August is an organization on the cutting edge of transparency. They believe that sharing pay information openly promotes honesty, credibility, and fairness.

We've all been conditioned to believe it's not appropriate to talk about pay in public or with our colleagues. Many organizations even create policies prohibiting you from talking with your colleagues about pay. There's a management belief that if everyone knew what everyone got paid, there would be an onslaught of arguments and conflict or potential lawsuits. That leads to an obvious question: What is there to hide? What do we need to be secret about? What are we doing that talking about it openly would cause harm for employees?

Openness and transparency at work lead to greater engagement, fairness, and collaboration, whereas secrecy leads to more frequent resignations. An insightful article from *Harvard Business Review* highlights these findings. In a survey of more than 70,000 US employees, researchers looked at the relationship between pay and engagement and discovered a few interesting nuances.[13] How people perceive their pay matters more than what they're actually paid. The more information individuals have about why they earn what they do, especially in relation to their peers, the less likely they are to quit. The main predictor of satisfaction and intention to leave, HBR finds, is whether an employee feels they are paid fairly. Yet even when people's compensation is in line with their value on the job market, two-thirds believe they are underpaid. Of that group, 60 percent report low job satisfaction and say they plan to look for a new job within six months. This is all based on their perception when they don't know the facts!

In contrast, the author found that even at companies that pay below market wages, such as at startups, if employees know why they're paid less than what they could earn elsewhere, 82 percent say they're satisfied with their jobs and plan to stick around.[14] Being honest and open about what pay means creates the opportunity for people to extend trust to an organization and have a good understanding of their value to the whole.

---

13   Dave Smith, "Most People Have No Idea Whether They're Paid Fairly," *Harvard Business Review*, December 2015, https://hbr.org/2015/10/most-people-have-no-idea-whether-theyre-paid-fairly.

14   Smith, "Most People Have No Idea."

Unfortunately, the key issue on many leader's minds is that they don't want to share how much they themselves are being paid. According to an Economic Policy Institute article, CEO pay continues to be very high and has grown far faster in recent decades than typical workers' pay.[15] Excessive CEO pay oftentimes means those economic gains are not going to everyday workers. Back in 1984, Peter Drucker wrote an essay suggesting CEO compensation should add up to no more than 20 times the rank-and-file wages for our workers.[16] That would be a 20:1 ratio. The 2016 CEO-to-worker compensation ratio is 271:1.[17] The radically unbalanced compensation dynamic is one of the most entrenched elements of our Industrial Era mindset. It results in secrecy and competition and keeps us stuck in an operating system of fear, not love. If you're afraid to openly talk about executive pay and compensation in general, ask yourself honestly: why?

Organizations such as August choose to operate fearlessly with pay transparency. Mike Arauz, one of the company's cofounders, spent an hour with me and a few colleagues to discuss why this move was so important to them. August's mission is to build movements that transform

15   Lawrence Mishel and Jessica Schieder, "CEO Pay Remains High Relative to the Pay of Typical Workers and High-Wage Earners," Economic Policy Institute, July 20, 2017, https://www.epi.org/publication/ceo-pay-remains-high-relative-to-the-pay-of-typical-workers-and-high-wage-earners/.

16   John A. Byrne and Lindsey Gerdes, "The Man Who Invented Management," *Business Week*, November 28, 2005, 97–102.

17   Mishel and Schieder, "CEO Pay Remains High."

how the world organizes, leads, and works. Their purpose is building high-performing teams for the world's most meaningful missions, and transparency made sense for that mission.

One of their core beliefs is that today's most valuable work depends on teams of people who work well together. They help leaders and organizations design new ways of working. That means they chose to operate from a place of transparency from their very inception. Mike is an enthusiastic supporter of pay transparency as a way to ensure fairness and minimize gender biases and other sources of bias. He would state that the top selling point for transparent compensation is that more access to more information makes better operations for an organization. The cost of labor is often the biggest expense in the business, and it's important for everyone to understand it. For August, transparency helps with prioritization and stops widely disproportioned compensation to top executives.

Other organizations also are paving this path. Buffer, another transparent pay organization, says their open pay system breeds high trust among their teams while holding them accountable to paying people fairly and without bias. For more information on either organizations' approach to pay transparency, check out the links below:

August's open compensation model: https://medium.

com/21st-century-organizational-development/
the-august-open-compensation-model-for-self-managed-
organizations-69f2c5d9649c.

Buffer's model: https://open.buffer.com/salary-formula/.

PERCOLAB

Transparency is a telltale indicator of love in action. It speaks directly to the absence of fear and willingness to create more freedom and autonomy. Organizations choose transparency on many different topics: financial statements, money in the bank, ownership, customer satisfaction, internal quality score, etc. Some share all of these.

The most innovative and, frankly, fun practice I've seen around transparency is from a company based out of Canada, France, and Belgium called Percolab.[18] They have a practice called Open Team Meetings. It's likely not what you think. Not only do they invite anyone from within the organization to join as they wish, they invite complete strangers to their company meetings.[19] I'll pause while you think about that for a moment.

---

18   Home page, Percolab, http://www.percolab.com/en/

19   Elizabeth Hunt, "What Are You Doing on Tuesday? Or Why Percolab Has Open Team Meetings," Medium.com, September 9, 2017, https://medium.com/percolab-droplets/well-why-dont-you-just-come-to-one-of-our-team-meetings-d892f408251d.

When team members run into others who show interest in what they do, maybe at a coffee shop or restaurant, they openly give them an invitation to observe and participate in organizational meetings. If you're like me, you're asking yourself, "Wait, won't they talk about financial information or performance metrics or employee challenges?" The answer is yes. They invite strangers anyway. Here is what they find, according to Elizabeth Hunt:

> To me and to probably everyone else at Percolab too, opening up our team meetings is a practical benefit to the organization, the generosity people show us by sharing their insights into our work is amazing. But opening our team meetings is also a meaningful symbolic act: we are a fractal of how we would like organizations to function in the world. Imagine, if governments and institutions and corporations and foundations and community organizations had as their base model meetings that were open, transparent, collaborative, and drew on collective intelligence?... Imagine that.[20]

Small practices can make a huge difference when it comes to transparency. Make meetings open door; anyone who has an interest or perspective to share can attend. Use

20 "What Are You Doing on Tuesday? Or Why Percolab Has Open Team Meetings," Percolab blog, accessed April 28, 2018, http://www.percolab.com/en/ what-are-you-doing-on-tuesday-or-why-percolab-has-open-team-meetings/.

technology to provide all employees an open source of information from operations to finance to new products and ventures. Take baby steps. Find one thing each month to share openly with your employees.

Transparency doesn't mean only sharing secret information—it is also about sharing good news, which we often forget. As much as we hold information to the chest when we're fearful it might harm us if it becomes public, we are also not at all well practiced in sharing celebrations or great achievements of our colleagues. Transparency simply requires creating a practice to share openly.

We oftentimes get so entrenched in the day to day, we forget to take a breath and celebrate the incredible things being achieved every day. The more positivity we can bring to light, the more good we can do in a genuine way, not inventing positivity for the sake of it, but really recognizing people for their contributions.

I think people are starved for honest and genuine recognition. Most people say that the one thing that matters most for them at work is feeling valued. Celebrating accomplishments and achievements shows individuals they are appreciated and valued, and unites and inspires teams in a way that data-driven financial numbers do not. The human connection creates soulful cultures.

BENEFIT CORPORATIONS

Do you want to take this love in action to the next level? Are you curious how you, as an Evolved Executive, can externally signal the importance of people as well as profit, culture community, and our planet? Let me introduce you to B Corporation.

> Certified B Corporations and benefit corporations are both leaders of a global movement to use business as a force for good. Both meet higher standards of accountability and transparency. Both create the opportunity to unlock our full human potential and creativity to use the power of business for the higher purpose of solving society's most challenging problems.[21]

Clearly, the existence of B Corporations is a great example of love in action. This movement resonates deeply with the work I'm doing. It illustrates in practice the belief that organizations can be amazing vehicles for meaning, purpose, and love in our lives.

B Corps have an inspiring vision for the future outlined in their declaration of interdependence. One statement says, "This economy is comprised of a new type of organization, the B Corporation, which is purpose driven and creates

---

21 "Certified B Corps and Benefit Corporations," Certified B Corporation, accessed May 9, 2018, https://www.bcorporation.net/what-are-b-corps/certified-b-corps-and-benefit-corporations.

benefits for all stakeholders, not just shareholders."[22] At a time when it feels like there are rising fears, insecurities, a lack of trust, and violence all around us, organizations such as these are taking responsibility to build a more inclusive, purpose-driven society.

The beliefs underpinning this movement will sound familiar given everything discussed in the book thus far. B Corps believe

- They must be the change they seek in the world.
- That all business ought to be conducted as if people and place matter.
- Through their products, practices, and profits, businesses should aspire to do no harm and benefit all.
- To do so requires they act with the understanding we are all dependent upon each other and thus responsible for each other and future generations.[23]

B Corps take all of us and the planet into consideration. They provide inspiration and hope that we can make a difference, that organizations can truly be powerful forces for good, meaning, joy, happiness, and love in our lives. I've begun the certification process, and I encourage you to take a look at this process yourself

---

22   "The B Corp Declaration," Certified B Corporation, accessed May 9, 2018, https://www.bcorporation.net/what-are-b-corps/the-b-corp-declaration.

23   "The B Corp Declaration."

at: https://www.bcorporation.net/become-a-b-corp/
how-to-become-a-b-corp.

Conclusion

STEPPING INTO LOVE

Be brave enough to start a conversation that matters.

—MARGARET WHEATLEY

I believe in a world of work that is brimming with meaning and opportunities for growth. An organization that is a positive force for good in the world. A day when the vast majority of people are excited to dive into their workday and go home as energized as they entered the day. Maybe, just maybe, we aren't as far from this day as I once thought.

As I've moved through my own journey of writing this book, I've come across amazing leaders and organizations that give me true hope and inspiration. I've seen practices transform how people engage with their work and one another. I've seen immense change when individuals choose to let go of their fear and embrace the opportunity to design their leadership—from a place of love, purpose, and values. The future of work is now, and we have a tremendous opportunity to transform the landscape of business going forward.

ROAD AHEAD

The road ahead is not necessarily easy or clearly marked. As we embark on a journey of evolution, one thing is certain: we will change. However, because you have read this book, I know you have the radical courage you need to walk this path. You have the willingness to be different, to be bold, to try a new and different way of leading for all to see. You are willing to accept you might be ridiculed for being different, but it's the choice most authentic and sincere to who you are and what you want to create in this world. I honor you for this.

My husband often says, "Can you give up the good for the great?" It's a fitting question here. Are you willing to let go of what you have in the pursuit of something greater? To let go of what you know today to embrace your belief that tomorrow can be better? This is a deep question as you map out your next steps. It's human nature to hold on to what we know with tight hands for fear of the unknown. To grow, however, we must be willing to let go, to experience the surrender of not knowing the answer or the path ahead.

Letting go of our past beliefs and prior habits of leading is hard, but also soulfully liberating. You feel tremendous freedom as you let go of the fear and belief systems holding you back. When you walk through the other side after the long struggle, the world opens up to you. Freedom will wash over you, and you'll say, "I can't believe it took me this long to make a change. I didn't realize it was like this on the other side." Keep going! A life more aligned with purpose, passion, meaning, inspiration, and energy is built on the ashes of what we thought we knew. Having the courage to face and discard our assumptions is the hardest and most fulfilling thing we will ever do.

The implications for this change are greater now than ever. We are only beginning to realize that it will require a much different leader to get us to the next stage of business. Leading an evolved organization means living in a much more conscious way—not just about the environment and planet, but being awake to the implications for the human, social, and economic issues we are facing at work and in the world in general. Creating a new future will require new beliefs, new practices, and new organizational structures that allow for our humanness and wholeness to come alive at work. The birth of this book is in pursuit of this audacious goal.

Evolved Executives inherently believe employees instinctively have good intentions and will act in alignment with an organization's shared goals. They believe in operating from the power of purpose and human growth. They recognize our need for human connection and, at the same time, can see how fear can, if given the opportunity, sabotage our efforts of community. Lastly, these executives realize change begins within. Only when we embrace our own weaknesses, blind spots, and fear can we create a new way of working. By doing so, leaders can then build cultures that give people back their freedom to activate their own agency and cocreate a workplace where they are proud to be and are energized.

The practices within this book chart a journey into self-awareness that allows for you to expand your consciousness and, in turn, evolve your leadership. With such increases, you can then catalyze massive change and healing in our teams and organizations. This change happens one evolved leader at a time. The future of work is full of opportunity for greater meaning, fulfillment, purpose, and love—we just have to invest the effort and the courage to evolve.

A LABOR OF LOVE

I've shared the story of my own process of going through the traditional climb up the corporate ladder and my growing frustration and cynicism about the ways we work. I had to reinvent myself—a scary process that involved letting go of everything I thought I was and everything I thought it meant to be successful. It's been incredibly challenging, but also the most gratifying path I've ever been on. Today, I get to design the life I dreamed of living and continue to reinvent myself. I am privileged to work with organizations that have a desire to be truly great forces in the world. I'm able to bring my experience to help leaders who want to create environments where people thrive and grow and help them achieve these transitions.

I stand on the shoulders of incredible researchers, practitioners, and thought leaders in this field of study. I consider myself a vessel in many ways for the ideas presented in this book. I feel honored to learn with individuals who are far more knowledgeable, well-known, and celebrated than myself. I sit in a beautiful space where I have the opportunity to read, absorb, practice, iterate, and share ideas from this ecosystem, and to give back to those who desire to create a new future and implement these practices into reality. I am not the owner of these ideas, but one who has the chance to share, connect, cocreate, participate, and contribute to the important work of a worldwide movement. It really is a labor of love and gratitude for all those who have done this before and are doing it now in an effort of creating a more human and meaningful experience of work.

My purpose is to awake the souls of leaders to create soulful organizations. It's my passion to work with others who truly understand their calling to build love-based and/or purpose-based organizations. I have the amazing opportunity to get to know people in my coaching and consulting practices deeply, and join with them on the journey to create evolved organizations that serve the world in countless ways. Fortunately, the movement has begun, and more and more leaders recognize their desire and responsibility to create organizations as a powerful force for good. Together, we all are building a love-based future of work.

LOVE IN ACTION—CAN WE CHANGE THE WORLD?

The fundamental human ability to choose a different path forward can change your life and the world. You have the choice to maintain the status quo as well as the choice to do something different. We need leaders today to take bold action, to have an intolerance for the status quo, to actively find opportunities to embrace love over fear, and to create a new reality. We must recognize the impact leaders and organizational culture have on our individual and collective well-being. I believe love in action can change the world. Are you ready?

AGENDA FOR ACTION

I'm often asked, who do you work with? It is an interesting

question and is one I will answer with a series of questions. Think about this: Are you frustrated with the dysfunction of outdated management practices? Is your heart telling you it's time to change, but your head is keeping you stuck? Do you know in your heart that there has to be a better way to lead, to inspire, to be in relationship with our work? Would you classify yourself as an untraditional leader, one who believes in the value of human connection and joy at work? Or, have you gotten to such a point where you are about to say, "Screw this. I'm going to do something different because what I'm doing right now doesn't work." If you said yes to any of these statements, you are the kind of leader I work with.

You don't have to walk this journey alone. A trusted support system is essential to guide and encourage you, to give you resources and practices, but also the truth. I and my consulting practice work daily with people just like you going through this difficult journey toward love in action.

Untethered Consulting is named for a very specific reason, as "untether" means "letting go." We need to let go of our attachment to the old ways of being and operating at work. We can make a purposeful effort to awaken our soul to guide us in a new direction—one more in tune with our true nature and purpose. Only then can we step into the new future of possibility and wholeheartedness.

I've walked the path you're walking now myself, and I've been highly trained in both leadership development and transformational leadership. I offer coaching and consulting, resources, and tools you'll find tremendously helpful along the way. Untethered Consulting works primarily with executives and senior leaders who are dedicated and committed to creating a different way of being at work defined by love. We would be honored to work with you as well.

My best advice is to not go it alone. It is isolating to do it all by yourself. It can be daunting when you don't know what to expect and don't have the resources laid out in front of you so you can continue to move forward. It's an uphill battle to face change and rewire beliefs. Having a partner in the journey gives you strength along the way.

My best advice? Ask for help!

Untethered Consulting
Email: heather@untetheredconsulting.com
www.untetheredconsulting.com

Acknowledgments

I have such deep gratitude for so many people who have made this journey possible. First and foremost, to my husband and partner in crime, Colby Wickman. I would literally not be here without your support, encouragement, and love. Thank you for the endless conversations, for being you, and not letting me be anything less than me.

Thank you to all of my incredible colleagues who have supported me in this process. To Pete, for taking the time to connect and being such a trusted thought partner. To Ilene, who refused to let me get off the hook on writing this book. To Jack, for paving the way and allowing me a chance to learn with and from you. To Angie, for the endless hours of support and encouragement. To Katie, for believing in me and making sure we carve out time for fun. To my soul coach Melissa. Thank you for guiding me back to myself.

I owe a debt of gratitude to Susan Basterfield and the LeadWise Academy. Susan, you have been an instrumental teacher, mentor and resource. Who knew a random meeting a short year ago would have such a deep and profound impact? Thank you for being a pioneer in all you do.

Thank you to everyone on the Scribe team who helped me get these seemingly crazy ideas into the book it is today. Special thanks to Tom for your guidance with the original outline. Alex, I have such deep appreciation for your endless hours helping me refine these ideas as my thinking evolved. Lastly, thank you Julie, my incredible publisher who made all the pieces come together.

I have huge gratitude to all of the organizations identified in this book—including Decurion, Scribe, Percolab, and August—and the leaders who are taking bold moves to accomplish good in the world for all of us to learn from.

To Mom and Dad, thank you for raising a strong and fiercely independent woman. I know I've stressed you out with my oftentimes bizarre life decisions, but you have always let me live my life on my own terms. Thank you for your support and encouragement for me to be me.

Cheers to making memories and figuring out, "what the hell are we going to do now?"

And most of all, dear reader, I am grateful for you and the courage you have to choose the path of love!

About the Author

HEATHER HANSON WICKMAN, PHD, successfully climbed the corporate ladder in healthcare before charting a new path to support senior leaders in evolving their leadership and building soulful organizations. She specializes in organizational change and executive coaching, through which she has coached leaders on evolved business practices, deep self-awareness, and leadership development.

Heather has a bachelor's in human resource development, a master's in human resources and industrial relations, and a PhD in organizational systems. She has a passion for supporting organizations as they transition from traditional beliefs and practices to flexible, adaptable, and conscious ways of work. She has witnessed profound transformation in organizational leaders across the C-Suite. Find out more at UntetheredConsulting.com.

Made in the USA
San Bernardino, CA
07 July 2018